FIFINE AT THE FAIR,

AND OTHER POEMS.

BY

ROBERT BROWNING.

BOSTON:
JAMES R. OSGOOD & COMPANY,
(LATE TICKNOR & FIELDS, AND FIELDS, OSGOOD, & CO.)
1872.

[FROM ADVANCE SHEETS.]

Rand, Avery, & Co., Stereotypers and Printers, Boston.

CONTENTS.

FIFINE AT THE FAIR.

Done Elvire.

Vous plaît-il, don Juan, nous éclaircir ces beaux mystères ?

Don Juan.

Madame, à vous dire la vérité . . .

Done Elvire.

Ah ! que vous savez mal vous défendre pour un homme de cour, et qui doit être accoutumé à ces sortes de choses ! J'ai pitié de vous voir la confusion que vous avez. Que ne vous armez-vous le front d'une noble effronterie ? Que ne me jurez-vous que vous êtes toujours dans les mêmes sentimens pour moi, que vous m'aimez toujours avec une ardeur sans égale, et que rien n'est capable de vous détacher de moi que la mort ? — *Molière, Don Juan*, Act 1ier. Scène 3e.

DONNA ELVIRA.

Don Juan, might you please to help one give a guess,
Hold up a candle, clear this fine mysteriousness?

DON JUAN.

Madam, if needs I must declare the truth, — in short . . .

DONNA ELVIRA.

Fie! for a man of mode, accustomed at the court
To such a style of thing, how awkwardly my lord
Attempts defence! You move compassion, — that's the word, —
Dumfoundered and chapfallen! Why don't you arm your brow
With noble impudence? Why don't you swear and vow
No sort of change is come to any sentiment
You ever had for me? Affection holds the bent;
You love me now as erst, with passion that makes pale
All ardor else: nor aught in nature can avail
To separate us two, save what, in stopping breath,
May, peradventure, stop devotion likewise, — death!

PROLOGUE.

AMPHIBIAN.

I.

THE fancy I had to-day, —
  Fancy which turned a fear!
I swam far out in the bay,
  Since waves laughed warm and clear.

II.

I lay and looked at the sun;
  The noon-sun looked at me:
Between us two, no one
  Live creature, that I could see.

III.

Yes! — there came floating by
Me, who lay floating too,
Such a strange butterfly! —
Creature as dear as new;

IV.

Because the membraned wings,
So wonderful, so wide,
So sun-suffused, were things
Like soul, and nought beside.

V.

A handbreadth overhead!
All of the sea my own,
It owned the sky instead:
Both of us were alone.

VI.

I never shall join its flight;
For nought buoys flesh in air.
If it touch the sea, good-night!
Death sure and swift waits there.

VII.

Can the insect feel the better
  For watching the uncouth play
Of limbs that slip the fetter,
  Pretend as they were not clay?

VIII.

Undoubtedly I rejoice
  That the air comports so well
With a creature which had the choice
  Of the land once. Who can tell?

IX.

What if a certain soul
  Which early slipped its sheath,
And has for its home the whole
  Of heaven, thus look beneath;

X.

Thus watch one, who, in the world
  Both lives, and likes life's way,
Nor wishes the wings unfurled
  That sleep in the worm, they say?

XI.

But sometimes, when the weather
  Is blue, and warm waves tempt
To free one's self of tether,
  And try a life exempt

XII.

From worldly noise and dust,
  In the sphere which overbrims
With passion and thought, — why, just
  Unable to fly, one swims!

XIII.

By passion and thought upborne,
  One smiles to one's self, "They fare
Scarce better, they need not scorn
  Our sea, who live in the air."

XIV.

Emancipate through passion
  And thought, with sea for sky,
We substitute, in a fashion,
  For heaven, poetry:

XV.

Which sea, to all intent,
  Gives flesh such noon-disport
As a finer element
  Affords the spirit-sort.

XVI.

Whatever they are, we seem ;
  Imagine the thing they know ;
All deeds they do, we dream :
  Can heaven be else but so ?

XVII.

And, meantime, yonder streak
  Meets the horizon's verge :
That is the land to seek,
  If we tire, or dread the surge, —

XVIII.

Land the solid and safe,
  To welcome again (confess !)
When, high and dry, we chafe
  The body, and don the dress.

XIX.

Does she look, pity, wonder,
  At one who mimics flight,
Swims, — heaven above, sea under,
  Yet always earth in sight?

FIFINE AT THE FAIR.

I.

OH, trip and skip, Elvire! Link arm in arm with me:
Like husband and like wife, together let us see
The tumbling-troop arrayed, the strollers on their stage
Drawn up and under arms, and ready to engage.

II.

Now, who supposed the night would play us such a prank?—
That what was raw and brown, rough pole and shaven plank,
Mere bit of hoarding, half by trestle propped, half tub,
Would flaunt it forth as brisk as butterfly from grub?

This comes of sun and air, of autumn afternoon,
And Pornic and Saint Gille, whose feast affords the boon, —
This scaffold turned parterre, this flower-bed in full blow,
Bateleurs, baladines! We shall not miss the show!
They pace and promenade; they presently will dance:
What good were else i' the drum and fife? O pleasant land of France!

III.

Who saw them make their entry? At wink of eve, be sure,
They love to steal a march, nor lightly risk the lure.
They keep their treasure hid, nor stale (improvident)
Before the time is ripe, each wonder of their tent, —
Yon six-legged sheep, to wit, and he who beats a gong,
Lifts cap, and waves salute, exhilarates the throng, —
Their ape of many years and much adventure, grim
And gray with pitying fools who find a joke in him.
Or, best, the human beauty, Mimi, Toinette, Fifine,
Tricot fines down if fat, padding plumps up if lean,

Ere, shedding petticoat, modesty, and such toys,
They bounce forth, squalid girls transformed to gamesome boys.

IV.

No, no, thrice, Pornic, no! Perpend the authentic tale!
'Twas not for every Gawain to gaze upon the Grail!
But whoso went his rounds when flew bat, flitted midge,
Might hear across the dusk — where both roads join the bridge,
Hard by the little port — creak a slow caravan,
A chimneyed house on wheels; so shyly-sheathed, began
To broaden out the bud, which, bursting unaware,
Now takes away our breath, queen-tulip of the Fair!

V.

Yet morning promised much; for, pitched and slung and reared
On terrace 'neath the tower, 'twixt tree and tree appeared
An airy structure: how the pennon from its dome,
Frenetic to be free, makes one red stretch for home! —

The home far and away, the distance where lives joy,
The cure, at once and ever, of world and world's annoy;
Since what lolls full in front, a furlong from the booth,
But ocean-idleness, sky-blue, and millpond-smooth?

VI.

Frenetic to be free! And do you know there beats
Something within my breast as sensitive? — repeats
The fever of the flag? My heart makes just the same
Passionate stretch, fires up for lawlessness, lays claim
To share the life they lead, — losels, who have and use
The hour what way they will, — applaud them, or abuse
Society, whereof myself am at the beck,
Whose call obey, and stoop to burden stiffest neck!

VII.

Why is it, that whene'er a faithful few combine
To cast allegiance off, play truant, nor repine,
Agree to bear the worst, forego the best in store
For us, who, left behind, do duty as of yore, —
Why is it, that, disgraced, they seem to relish life the more? —

Seem as they said, "We know a secret passing praise
Or blame of such as you! Remain! we go our ways
With something you o'erlooked, forgot, or chose to sweep
Clean out of door,—our pearl picked from your rubbish-heap.
You care not for your loss: we calculate our gain.
All's right. Are you content? Why, so let things remain!
To the wood then, to the wild: free life, full liberty!"
And when they rendezvous beneath the inclement sky,
House by the hedge, reduced to brute-companionship,—
Misguided ones who gave society the slip,
And find too late how boon a parent they despised,
What ministration spurned, how sweet and civilized,—
Then, left alone at last with self-sought wretchedness,
No interloper else! why is it—can we guess?—
At somebody's expense goes up so frank a laugh?
As though they held the corn, and left us only chaff
From garners crammed and closed; and we indeed are clever
If we get grain as good by thrashing straw forever.

VIII.

Still, truants as they are, and purpose yet to be,
That nowise needs forbid they venture — as you see —
To cross confine, approach the once familiar roof
O' the kindly race their flight estranged: half stand aloof,
Half sidle up, press near, and proffer wares for sale,
In their phrase; make, in ours, white levy of black mail.
They, of the wild, require some touch of us the tame;
Since clothing, meat, and drink mean money all the same.

IX.

If hunger, proverbs say, allures the wolf from wood,
Much more the bird must dare a dash at something good;
Must snatch up, bear away in beak, the trifle-treasure
To wood and wild, and then — oh, how enjoy at leisure!
Was never tree-built nest, you climbed and took, of bird,
(Rare city-visitant, talked of, scarce seen or heard,)
But, when you would dissect the structure piece by piece,
You found inwreathed amid the country-product — fleece

And feather, thistle-fluffs and bearded windlestraws —
Some shred of foreign silk, unravelling of gauze,
Bit, maybe, of brocade, 'mid fur and thistle-down ;
Filched plainly from mankind, dear tribute paid by town,
Which proved how oft the bird had plucked up heart of
grace,
Swooped down at waif and stray, made furtively our place
Pay tax and toll, then borne the booty to enrich
Her paradise i' the waste ; the how and why of which,
That is the secret, there the mystery that stings.

X.

For what they traffic in consists of just the things
We proud ones who so scorn dwellers without the pale,
Bateleurs, baladines, white leviers of black mail, —
I say, they sell what we most pique us that we keep :
How comes it, all we hold so dear they count so cheap ?

XI.

What price should you impose, for instance, on repute,
Good fame, your own good fame and family's to boot ?

Stay start of quick mustache, arrest the angry rise
Of eyebrow! All I asked is answered by surprise.
Now tell me: are you worth the cost of a cigar?
Go boldly, enter booth, disburse the coin at bar
Of doorway where presides the master of the troop,
And forthwith you survey his Graces in a group, —
Live picture, picturesque no doubt, and close to life:
His sisters, right and left; the Grace in front, his wife.
Next, who is this performs the feat of the trapeze?
Lo, she is launched: look, fie, the fairy! — how she flees
O'er all those heads thrust back! — mouths, eyes, one gape and stare.
No scrap of skirt impedes free passage through the air,
Till, plumb on the other side, she lights, and laughs again, —
That fairy-form, whereof each muscle, nay, each vein,
The curious may inspect, — his daughter that he sells
Each rustic for five sous. Desiderate aught else
O' the vender? As you leave his show, — why, joke the man: —
"You cheat: your six-legged sheep, I recollect, began

Both life and trade, last year, trimmed properly and clipt
As the Twin-headed Babe and Human Nondescript."
What does he care? You paid his price, may pass your jest.
So values he repute, good fame, and all the rest.

XII.

But try another tack: say, "I indulge caprice,
Who am Don and Duke, and Knight, beside, o' the Golden Fleece,
And never mind how rich. Abandon this career;
Have hearth and home; nor let your womankind appear
Without as multiplied a coating as protects
An onion from the eye; become, in all respects,
God-fearing householder, subsistent by brain-skill,
Hand-labor; win your bread whatever way you will,
So it be honestly, — and, while I have a purse,
Means shall not lack:" his thanks will be the roundest curse
That ever rolled from lip.

XIII.

Now, what is it—returns
The question—heartens so this losel, that he spurns
All we so prize? I want put down in black and white
What compensating joy, unknown and infinite,
Turns lawlessness to law, makes destitution wealth,
Vice virtue, and disease of soul and body health.

XIV.

Ah the slow shake of head, the melancholy smile,
The sigh almost a sob! What's wrong, was right erewhile?
Why are we two at once such ocean-width apart?
Pale fingers press my arm, and sad eyes probe my heart.
Why is the wife in trouble?

XV.

This way, this way, Fifine!
Here's she shall make my thoughts be surer what they mean!
First let me read the signs, portray you past mistake
The gypsy's foreign self, no swarth our sun could bake.

Yet where's a woolly trace, degrades the wiry hair?
And note the Greek-nymph nose, and — oh, my Hebrew pair
Of eye and eye, — o'erarched by velvet of the mole, —
That swim as in a sea, that dip and rise and roll,
Spilling the light around! while either ear is cut
Thin as a dusk-leaved rose carved from a cocoa-nut.
And then her neck! — now, grant you had the power to deck,
Just as your fancy pleased, the bistre-length of neck;
Could lay, to shine against its shade, a moon-like row
Of pearl, each round and white as bubble Cupids blow
Big out of mother's milk: what pearl-moon would surpass
That string of mock-turquoise, those almandines of glass,
Where girlhood terminates? for with breasts'-birth commence
The boy, and page-costume, till pink and impudence
End admirably all: complete, the creature trips
Our way now, brings sunshine upon her spangled hips,
As here she fronts us full, with pose half frank, half fierce!

XVI.

Words urged in vain, Elvire! You waste your carte and tierce,
Lunge at a phantom here, try fence in fairy-land.
For me, I own defeat; ask but to understand
The acknowledged victory of whom I call my queen,
Sexless and bloodless sprite: though mischievous and mean,
Yet free and flower-like too, with loveliness for law,
And self-sustainment made morality.

XVII.

A flaw
Do you account i' the lily, of lands which travellers know,
That, just as a golden gloom supersedes northern snow
I' the chalice, so, about each pistil, spice is packed,
Deliriously-drugged scent, in lieu of odor lacked,
With us, by bee and moth, their banquet to enhance
At morn and eve, when dew, the chilly sustenance,
Needs mixture of some chaste and temperate perfume?
I ask, is she in fault who guards such golden gloom,

Such dear and damning scent, by who cares what
devices,
And takes the idle life of insects she entices,
When, drowned to heart's desire, they satiate the inside
O' the lily, mark her wealth, and manifest her pride?

XVIII.

But, wiser, we keep off, nor tempt the acrid juice;
Discreet we peer and praise, put rich things to right
use.
No flavorous venomed bell, — the rose it is, I wot,
Only the rose, we pluck and place, unwronged a jot,
No worse for homage done by every devotee,
I' the proper loyal throne, on breast where rose should
be.
Or if the simpler sweets we have to choose among
Would taste between our teeth, and give its toy the
tongue, —
O gorgeous poison-plague! on thee no hearts are set;
We gather daisy meek, or maiden violet:
I think it is Elvire we love, and not Fifine.

XIX.

"How does she make my thoughts be sure of what they mean?"
Judge, and be just! Suppose an age and time long past
Renew for our behoof one pageant more, the last
O' the kind, sick Louis liked to see defile between
Him and the yawning grave its passage served to screen.
With eye as gray as lead, with cheek as brown as bronze,
Here where we stand, shall sit and suffer Louis Onze;
The while from yonder tent parade forth, not—oh, no!—
Bateleurs, baladines, but range themselves a-row
Those well-sung women-worthies whereof loud fame still finds
Some echo linger faint, less in our hearts than minds.

XX.

See, Helen! pushed in front o' the world's worst night and storm
By Lady Venus' hand on shoulder; the sweet form
Shrinkingly prominent, though mighty, like a moon
Outbreaking from a cloud, to put harsh things in tune,

And magically bring mankind to acquiesce
In its own ravage, — call no curse upon, but bless
(Beldam a moment since) the outbreaking beauty, now,
That casts o'er all the blood a candor from her brow.
See, Cleopatra! bared, the entire and sinuous wealth
O' the shining shape; each orb of indolent ripe health,
Captured, just where it finds a fellow-orb as fine
I' the body; traced about by jewels which outline,
Fire-frame, and keep distinct, perfections, lest they melt
To soft smooth unity ere half their hold be felt:
Yet, o'er that white and wonder, a soul's predominance
I' the head so high and haught, except one thievish glance,
From back of oblong eye, intent to count the slain.
Hush, oh! I know, Elvire! Be patient; more remain.
What say you to Saint — pish! whatever saint you please,
Cold-pinnacled aloft o' the spire, prays calm the seas
From Pornic church, and oft at midnight (peasants say)
Goes walking out to save from shipwreck: well she may;

For think how many a year has she been conversant
With nought but winds and rains, sharp courtesy, and scant
O' the wintry snow that coats the pent-house of her shrine,
Covers each knee, climbs near, but spares the smile benign
Which seems to say, "I looked for scarce so much from earth."
She follows, one long, thin pure finger in the girth
O' the girdle, whence the folds of garment, eye and eye,
Besprent with fleur-de-lis, flow down and multiply
Around her feet; and one pressed hushingly to lip,
As if, while thus we made her march, some foundering ship
Might miss her from her post, nearer to God half-way
In heaven; and she thought, "Who that treads earth can pray?
I doubt if even she, the unashamed! though, sure,
She must have stripped herself only to clothe the poor."

XXI.

This time, enough's a feast, not one more form, Elvire!
Provided you allow, that, bringing up the rear
O' the bevy I am loath to — by one bird — curtail,
First note may lead to last, an octave crown the scale,
And this feminity be followed — do not flout! —
By — who concludes the mask with courtesy, smile, and pout,
Submissive-mutinous? No other than Fifine
Points toe, imposes haunch, and pleads with tambourine.

XXII.

"Well, what's the meaning here, what does the mask intend,
Which, unabridged, we saw file past us, with no end
Of fair ones, till Fifine came, closed the catalogue?"

XXIII.

Task fancy yet again. Suppose you cast this clog
Of flesh away (that weeps, upbraids, withstands my arm),
And pass to join your peers; paragon charm with charm,

As I shall show you may; prove best of beauty there;
Yourself confront yourself. This help me to declare,
That yonder-you, who stand beside these, braving each,
And blinking none, beat her who lured to Troy-town beach
The purple prows of Greece; nay, beat Fifine, whose face
Mark how I will inflame, when seigneur-like I place
I' the tambourine, to spot the strained and piteous blank
Of pleading parchment, see, no less than a whole franc!

XXIV.

Ah! do you mark the brown o' the cloud, made bright with fire
Through and through? as, old wiles succeeding to desire,
Quality (you and I) once more compassionate
A hapless infant, doomed (fie on such partial fate!)
To sink the inborn shame, waive privilege of sex,
And posture as you see, support the nods and becks

Of clowns that have their stare, nor always pay its price;
An infant born, perchance, as sensitive and nice
As any soul of you, proud dames, whom destiny
Keeps uncontaminate from stigma of the sty
She wallows in! You draw back skirts from filth like her,
Who possibly braves scorn, if, scorned, she minister
To age, want, and disease of parents one or both;
Nay, peradventure, stoops to degradation, loath
That some just budding sister, the dew yet on the rose,
Should have to share in turn the ignoble trade: who knows?

XXV.

Ay, who indeed! Myself know nothing, but dare guess
That off she trips in haste to hand the booty — yes,
'Twixt fold and fold of tent there looms he, dim discerned,
The ogre, lord of all — those lavish limbs have earned!

Brute-beast-face — ravage, scar, scowl, and malig-
nancy —
O' the Strong Man, whom (no doubt, her husband) by
and by
You shall behold do feats, — lift up, nor quail beneath,
A quintal in each hand, a cart-wheel 'twixt his teeth.
Oh! she prefers sheer strength to ineffective grace,
Breeding, and culture; seeks the essential in the case.
To him has flown my franc; and welcome, if that squint
O' the diabolic eye so soften, through absinthe,
That, for once, tambourine, tunic, and tricot 'scape
Their customary curse, "Not half the gain of the ape!"
Ay, they go in together.

XXVI.

Yet still her phantom stays
Opposite, where you stand as steady 'neath our gaze, —
The live Elvire's and mine, — though fancy-stuff and
mere
Illusion, to be judged, — dream-figures, — without fear
Or favor, those the false, by you and me the true.

XXVII.

"What puts it in my head to make yourself judge you?"
Well, it may be the name of Helen brought to mind
A certain myth I mused in years long left behind:
How she that fled from Greece with Paris, whom she loved,
And came to Troy, and there found shelter, and so proved
Such cause of the world's woe,—how she, old stories call
This creature, Helen's self, never saw Troy at all.
Jove had his fancy-fit; must needs take empty air,
Fashion her likeness forth, and set the phantom there
I' the midst for sport, to try conclusions with the blind
And blundering race, the game create for gods, mankind:
Experiment on these; establish who would yearn
To give up life for her, who, other-minded, spurn
The best her eyes could smile; make half the world sublime,
And half absurd, for just a phantom all the time!

Meanwhile true Helen's self sat, safe and far away,
By a great river-side, beneath a purer day,
With solitude around, tranquillity within;
Was able to lean forth, look, listen, through the din
And stir; could estimate the worthlessness or worth
Of Helen, who inspired such passion to the earth,
A phantom all the time! That put it in my head
To make yourself judge you, — the phantom-wife, instead
O' the tearful, true Elvire.

XXVIII.

I thank the smile at last
Which thins away the tear. Our sky was overcast,
And something fell; but day clears up: if there chanced rain,
The landscape glistens more. I have not vexed in vain
Elvire; because she knows, now she has stood the test,
How, this and this being good, herself may still be best
O' the beauty in review; because the flesh that claimed
Unduly my regard, she thought, the taste she blamed

In me for things externe, was all mistake, she finds,
Or will find when I prove that bodies show me minds;
That, through the outward sign, the inward grace allures,
And sparks from heaven transpierce earth's coarsest covertures, —
All by demonstrating the value of Fifine!

XXIX.

Partake my confidence. No creature's made so mean,
But that, some way, it boasts, could we investigate,
Its supreme worth; fulfils, by ordinance of fate,
Its momentary task; gets glory all its own;
Tastes triumph in the world, pre-eminent, alone.
Where is the single grain of sand, 'mid millions heaped
Confusedly on the beach, but, did we know, has leaped,
Or will leap would we wait, i' the century, some once,
To the very throne of things? — earth's brightest for the nonce,
When sunshine shall impinge on just that grain's facette
Which fronts him fullest, first, returns his ray with jet

Of promptest praise, thanks God best in creation's name.
As firm is my belief, quick sense perceives the same
Self-vindicating flash illustrate every man
And woman of our mass, and prove, throughout the plan,
No detail, but, in place allotted it, was prime
And perfect.

XXX.

Witness her, kept waiting all this time!
What happy angle makes Fifine reverberate
Sunshine,—least sand-grain, she, of shadiest social state?
No adamantine shield, polished like Helen there,
Fit to absorb the sun, regorge him till the glare,
Dazing the universe, draw Troy-ward those blind beaks
Of equal-sided ships rowed by the well-greaved Greeks.
No Asian mirror like yon Ptolematic witch
Able to fix sun fast, and tame sun down, enrich,
Not burn, the world with beams thus flatteringly rolled
About her, head to foot, turned slavish snakes of gold!

And, oh! no tinted pane of oriel sanctity
Does our Fifine afford, such as permits supply
Of lustrous heaven, revealed, far more than mundane sight
Could master, to thy cell, pure saint! where, else too bright,
So suits thy sense the orb, that what outside was noon
Pales through thy lozenged blue to meek benefic moon!
What then?—does that prevent each dunghill we may pass
Daily from boasting, too, its bit of looking-glass,
Its sherd, which, sun-smit, shines, shoots arrowy fire beyond
That satin-muffled mope, your sulky diamond?

XXXI.

And, now, the mingled ray she shoots I decompose.
Her antecedents take for execrable! Gloze
No whit on your premise: let be there was no worst
Of degradation spared Fifine, ordained from first
To last, in body and soul, for one life-long debauch,—
The Pariah of the North, the European Nautch!

This, far from seek to hide, she puts in evidence
Calmly, displays the brand, bids pry without offence
Your finger on the place. You comment, "Fancy us
So operated on, maltreated, mangled thus!
Such torture in our case, had we survived an hour?
Some other sort of flesh and blood must be, with power
Appropriate to the vile, unsensitive, tough-thonged,
In lieu of our fine nerve! Be sure she was not wronged
Too much: you must not think she winced at prick as we!"
Come, come, that's what you say; or would, were thoughts but free.

XXXII.

Well then, thus much confessed, what wonder if there steal
Unchallenged to my heart the force of one appeal
She makes, and justice stamp the sole claim she asserts?
So absolutely good is truth, truth never hurts
The teller, whose worst crime gets somehow grace, avowed.
To me, that silent pose and prayer proclaimed aloud,

"Know all of me outside: the rest be emptiness
For such as you! I call attention to my dress,
Coiffure, outlandish features, and memorable limbs,
Piquant entreaty, all that eye-glance overskims.
Does this much pleasure? Then repay the pleasure; put
Its price i' the tambourine! Do you seek farther? Tut!
I'm just my instrument,—sound hollow; mere smooth skin
Stretched o'er gilt framework, I: rub-dub, nought else within—
Always, for such as you!—if I have use elsewhere;
If certain bells, now mute, can jingle, need you care?
Be it enough, there's truth i' the pleading, which comports
With no word spoken out in cottages or courts;
Since all I plead is, 'Pay for just the sight you see,
And give no credit to another charm in me.'
Do I say, like your love, 'To praise my face is well;
But who would know my worth must search my heart *to tell*'?

Do I say, like your wife ? — 'Had I passed in review
The produce of the globe, my man of men were — you !'
Do I say, like your Helen ? — 'Yield yourself up, obey
Implicitly, nor pause to question, to survey
Even the worshipful ; prostrate you at my shrine :
Shall you dare controvert what the world counts divine ?
Array your private taste, own liking of the sense,
Own longing of the soul, against the impudence
Of history, the blare and bullying of verse ?
As if man ever yet saw reason to disburse
The amount of what sense liked, soul longed for, — given, devised
As love, forsooth, — until the price was recognized
As moderate enough by divers fellow-men !
Then, with his warrant safe that these would love too, then,
Sure that particular gain implies a public loss,
And that no smile he buys but proves a slash across
The face, a stab into the side of somebody ;
Sure that, along with love's main purchase, he will buy
Up the whole stock of earth's uncharitableness,
Envy and hatred, — then decides he to profess

His estimate of one love had discerned, though dim
To all the world beside: since what's the world to
 him?'
Do I say, like your Queen of Egypt?—'Who foregoes
My cup of witchcraft—fault be on the fool! He
 knows
Nothing of how I pack my wine-press, turn its winch
Three times three, all the time to song and dance, nor
 flinch
From charming on and on, till at the last I squeeze
Out the exhaustive drop that leaves behind mere lees
And dregs, vapidity, thought essence heretofore!
Sup of my sorcery, old pleasures please no more!
Be great, be good, love, learn, have potency of hand
Or heart or head,—what boots? You die, nor under-
 stand
What bliss might be in life: you ate the grapes, but
 knew
Never the taste of wine, such vintage as I brew!'
Do I say, like your saint?—'An exquisitest touch
Bides in the birth of things: no after-time can much

Enhance that fine, that faint, fugitive first of all!
What color paints the cup o' the May-rose like the small
Suspicion of a blush which doubtfully begins?
What sound out-warbles brook, while, at the source, it
wins
That moss and stone dispart, allow its bubblings breathe?
What taste excels the fruit, just where sharp flavors
sheathe
Their sting, and let encroach the honey that allays?
And so with soul and sense: when sanctity betrays
First fear lest earth below seem real as heaven above,
And holy worship, late, change soon to sinful love,
Where is the plenitude of passion which endures
Comparison with that, I ask of amateurs?'
Do I say, like Elvire"—

XXXIII.

(Your husband holds you fast,
Will have you listen, learn your character at last!)—
"Do I say?—like her mixed unrest and discontent,
Reproachfulness and scorn, with that submission blent

So strangely in the face by sad smiles and gay tears, —
Quiescence which attacks, rebellion which endears, —
Say? — 'As you love me once, could you but love me now!
Years probably have graved their passage on my brow,
Lips turn more rarely red, eyes sparkle less than erst;
Such tribute body pays to time: but, unamerced,
The soul retains, nay, boasts old treasure multiplied.
Though dew-prime flee, — mature at noonday, love defied
Chance, the wind, change, the rain; love, strenuous all the more
For storm, struck deeper root, and choicer fruitage bore,
Despite the rocking world. Yet truth struck root in vain:
While tenderness bears fruit, you praise, not taste again.
Why? They are yours, which once were hardly yours, might go
To grace another's ground; and then — the hopes we know,
The fears we keep in mind! when, ours to arbitrate,
Your part was to bow neck, bid fall decree of fate.

Then, oh the knotty point! — white-night's work to revolve, —
What meant that smile, that sigh? Not Solon's self could solve!
Then, oh the deep surmise what one word might express!
And if what sounded "No" may not have echoed "Yes!"
Then such annoy could cause cold welcome, such acquist
Of rapture, that, refused the arm, hand touched the wrist!
Now, what's a smile to you? Poor candle that lights up
The decent household gloom which sends you out to sup.
A tear? worse! warns that health requires you keep aloof
From nuptial chamber, since rain penetrates the roof!
For all is got and gained, inalienably safe,
Your own, and, so, despised; more worth has any waif
Or stray from neighbor's pale: pouch that, — 'tis pleasure, pride,
Novelty, property, and larceny beside!

Preposterous thought! to find no value fixed in things;
To covet all you see, hear, dream of, till fate brings
About, that, what you want, you get; then comes a
change.
Give you the sun to keep, forthwith must fancy range:
A goodly lamp, no doubt; yet might you catch her hair,
And capture, as she frisks, the fen-fire dancing there!
What do I say? at least, a meteor's half in heaven:
Provided filth but shine, my husband hankers even
After putridity that's phosphorescent; cribs
The rustic's tallow-rush; makes spoil of urchins' squibs;
In short, prefers to me — chaste, temperate, serene —
What sputters green and blue, this fizgig called Fifine!'"

XXXIV.

So all your sex mistake! Strange that so plain a
fact
Should raise such dire debate! Few families were
racked
By torture self-supplied, did Nature grant but this, —
That women comprehend mental analysis!

XXXV.

Elvire, do you recall when, years ago, our home
The intimation reached, a certain pride of Rome,
Authenticated piece, in the third, last, and best
Manner, — whatever fools and connoisseurs contest, —
No particle disturbed by rude restorer's touch,
The palaced picture-pearl, so long eluding clutch
Of creditor, at last the Raphael might — could we
But come to terms — change lord, pass from the prince to me?
I think you recollect my fever of a year;
How the prince would, and how he would not: now, too dear
That promise was he made his grandsire so long since, —
Rather to boast "I own a Raphael" than "am prince!"
And now, the fancy soothed, — if really sell he must
His birthright for a mess of pottage, — such a thrust
T' the vitals of the prince were mollified by balm,
Could he prevail upon his stomach to bear qualm,
And bequeath Liberty (because a purchaser
Was ready with the sum, — a trifle!); yes, transfer

His heart, at all events, to that land where, at least,
Free institutions reign! And so, its price increased
Fivefold (Americans are such importunates!),
Soon must his Raphael start for the United States.
Oh alternating bursts of hope, and then despair!
At last, the bargain's struck; I'm all but beggared: there
The Raphael faces me, in fine, no dream at all,
My housemate, evermore to glorify my wall.
A week I pass, before heart-palpitations sink,
In gloating o'er my gain, so lately on the brink
Of loss; a fortnight more I spend in paradise: —
"Was outline e'er so true, could coloring entice
So calm, did harmony and quiet so avail?
How right, how resolute, the action tells the tale!"
A month, I bid my friends congratulate their best: —
"You happy Don!" (to me) "The blockhead!" (to the
rest):
"No doubt he thinks his daub original, poor dupe!"
Then I resume my life: one chamber must not coop
My life in, though it boast a marvel like my prize.
This year, I saunter past with unaverted eyes;

Nay, loll and turn my back; perchance to overlook
With relish, leaf by leaf, Doré's last picture-book.

XXXVI.

Imagine that a voice reproached me from its frame:—
"Here do I hang, and may! Your Raphael, just the same;
'Tis only you that change: no ecstasies of yore!
No purposed suicide distracts you any more!"
Prompt would my answer turn such frivolous attack:—
"You misappropriate sensations. What I lack,
And labor to obtain, is hoped and feared about
After a fashion: what I once obtain, makes doubt,
Expectancy, old fret and fume, henceforward void.
But do I think to hold my havings unalloyed
By novel hope and fear, of fashion just as new,
To correspond i' the scale? Nowise, I promise you!
Mine you are, therefore mine will be, as fit to cheer
My soul and glad my sense to-day as this-day-year.
So, any sketch or scrap, pochade, caricature,
Made in a moment, meant a moment to endure,

I snap at, seize, and then forever throw aside,
And find you in your place. But if a servant cried
'Fire in the gallery!'—methinks, were I engaged
In Doré, elbow-deep, portfolios million-paged
To the four winds would pack, sped by the heartiest curse
Was ever launched from lip, to strew the universe;
While I would brave the best o' the burning, bear away
Either my perfect piece in safety, or else stay
And share its fate: if made a martyr, why repine?
Inextricably wed, such ashes mixed with mine!"

XXXVII.

For which I get the eye, the hand, the heart, the whole
O' the wondrous wife again!

XXXVIII.

But no: play out your rôle
I' the pageant! 'Tis not fit your phantom leave the stage:
I want you, there, to make you, here, confess you wage

Successful warfare, pique those proud ones, and advance
Claim to — equality? nay, but predominance
In physique o'er them all, where Helen heads the scene
Closed by its tiniest of tail-tips, pert Fifine.
How ravishingly pure you stand in pale constraint!
My new-created shape, without or touch or taint,
Inviolate of life and worldliness and sin, —
Fettered, I hold my flower, her own cup's weight would win
From off the tall slight stalk a-top of which she turns
And trembles, makes appeal to one who roughly earns
Her thanks instead of blame (did lily only know),
By thus constraining length of lily, letting snow
Of cup-crown, that's her face, look from its guardian stake,
Superb on all that crawls beneath, and mutely make
Defiance, with the mouth's white movement of disdain,
To all that stoops, retires, and hovers round again!
How windingly the limbs delay to lead up, reach
Where, crowned, the head waits calm! as if reluctant, each,

That eye should traverse quick such lengths of loveli-
ness,
From feet, which just are found embedded in the dress
Deep swathed about with folds and flowings virginal
Up to the pleated breasts, rebellious 'neath their pall,
As if the vesture's snow were moulding sleep, not death;
Must melt, and must release: whereat, from the fine
sheath,
The flower-cup-crown starts free, the face is unconcealed;
And what shall now divert, once the sweet face revealed,
From all I loved so long, so lingeringly left?

XXXIX.

Because, indeed, your face fits into just the cleft
O' the heart of me, Elvire; makes right and whole once
more
All that was half itself without you! As before,
My truant in its place! Because e'en sea-shells yearn,
Plundered by any chance: would have their pearl return,
Let negligently slip away into the wave!
Never may they desist, those eyes so gray and grave,

From their slow sure supply of the effluent soul within!
And — would you humor me? — I dare to ask, unpin
The web of that brown hair! O'erwash o' the sudden,
but
As promptly, too, disclose, on either side, the jut
Of alabaster brow! So part, those rillets dyed
Deep by the woodland leaf, when down they pour, each
side
O' the rock-top, pushed by Spring!

XL.

"And where i' the world is all
This wonder, I detail so trippingly, espied?
Your mirror would reflect a tall, thin, pale, deep-eyed
Personage, pretty once, it may be, doubtless still,
Loving, — a certain grace yet lingers, if I will, —
But all this wonder, where?"

XLI.

Why, where but in the sense
And soul of me, the judge of art? Art-evidence,

That thing was, is, might be; but no more thing itself
Than flame is fuel. Once the verse-book laid on shelf,
The picture turned to wall, the music fled from ear,
Each beauty, born of each, grows clearer and more clear,
Mine henceforth, ever mine!

XLII.

But if I would retrace
Effect in art to cause, corroborate, erase
What's right or wrong i' the lines, test fancy in my brain
By fact which gave it birth? I reperuse in vain
The verse; I fail to find that vision of delight
I' the Razzi's lost profile, eye-edge so exquisite.
And music: what? that burst of pillared cloud by day
And pillared fire by night was product, must we say,
Of modulating just by enharmonic change, —
The augmented sixth resolved, — from out the straighter range
Of D sharp minor, — leap of disimprisoned thrall, —
Into thy light and life, D major natural?

XLIII.

Elvire, will you partake in what I shall impart?
I seem to understand the way heart chooses heart
By help of the outside face, — a reason for our wild
Diversity in choice, — why each grows reconciled
To what is absent, what superfluous in the mask:
Material meant to yield, — did Nature ply her task
As artist should, — precise the features of the soul;
Which, if in any case they found expression, whole
I' the traits, would give a type, undoubtedly display
A novel, true, distinct perfection in its way.
Never shall I believe any two souls were made
Similar: granting, then, each soul of every grade
Was meant to be itself, and in itself complete,
And in completion good, — nay, best o' the kind, — as meet
Needs must it be that show on the outside correspond
With inward substance, — flesh, the dress which soul has donned,
Exactly reproduce, — were only justice done
Inside and outside too, — types perfect every one.

How happens it that here we meet a mystery
Insoluble to man, a plaguy puzzle? Why
Either is each soul made imperfect, and deserves
As rude a face to match, or else a bungler swerves,
And Nature, on a soul worth rendering aright,
Works ill, or proves perverse, or, in her own despite,—
Here too much, there too little,—makes each face more or less
Retire from beauty, and approach to ugliness?
And yet succeeds the same: since, what is wanting to success,
If somehow every face, no matter how deform,
Evidence to some one of hearts on earth, that, warm
Beneath the veriest ash, there hides a spark of soul,
Which, quickened by love's breath, may yet pervade the whole
O' the gray, and, free again, be fire?—of worth the same,
Howe'er produced; for, great or little, flame is flame.
A mystery, whereof solution is to seek.

XLIV.

I find it in the fact that each soul, just as weak
Its own way as its fellow, — departure from design
As flagrant in the flesh, — goes striving to combine
With what shall right the wrong, the under or above
The standard ; supplement unloveliness by love.
Ask Plato else ! And this corroborates the sage,
That art, — which I may style the love of loving, rage
Of knowing, seeing, feeling the absolute truth of things
For truth's sake, whole and sole, nor any good truth brings
The knower, seer, feeler, beside, — instinctive art,
Must fumble for the whole, once fixing on a part,
However poor, surpass the fragment, and aspire
To reconstruct thereby the ultimate entire.
Art, working with a will, discards the superflux,
Contributes to defect, toils on, till — *fiat lux* —
There's the restored, the prime, the individual type !

XLV.

Look, for example, now ! This piece of broken pipe

(Some shipman's solace erst) shall act as crayon ; and
What tablet better serves my purpose than the sand ?—
Smooth slab whereon I draw, no matter with what skill,
A face, and yet another, and yet another still.
There lie my three prime types of beauty !

XLVI.

Laugh your best !
"Exaggeration and absurdity ?" Confessed !
Yet what may that face mean ?—no matter for its nose,
A yard long ; or its chin, a foot short.

XLVII.

"You suppose,
Horror ?" Exactly ! What's the odds, if, more or less
By yard or foot, the features do manage to express
Such meaning in the main ? Were I of Gerôme's force,
Nor feeble as you see, quick should my crayon course
O'er outline, curb, excite, till—so completion speeds
With Gerôme well at work—observe how brow recedes,

Head shudders back on spine, as if one haled the hair,
Would have the full-face front what pin-point eye's sharp
stare
Announces; mouth agape to drink the flowing fate,
While chin protrudes to meet the burst o' the wave: elate
Almost, spurred on to brave necessity, expend
All life left, in one flash, as fire does at its end.
Retrenchment and addition effect a masterpiece,
Not change i' the motive: here diminish, there increase;
And who wants Horror has it.

XLVIII.

Who wants some other show
Of soul may seek elsewhere,—this second of the row?
What does it give for germ, monadic mere intent
Of mind in face, faint first of meanings ever meant?
Why, possibly, a grin, that, strengthened, grows a laugh;
That, softened, leaves a smile; that, tempered, bids you
quaff
At such a magic cup as English Reynolds once
Compounded: for the witch pulls out of you response

Like Garrick's to Thalia, however due may be
Your homage claimed by that stiff-stoled Melpomene!

XLIX.

And just this one face more! Pardon the bold pretence!
May there not lurk some hint, struggle toward evidence,
In that compressed mouth, those strained nostrils, steadfast eyes
Of utter passion, absolute self-sacrifice,
Which — could I but subdue the wild grotesque, refine
That bulge of brow, make blunt that nose's aquiline,
And let, although compressed, a point of pulp appear
I' the mouth — would give at last the portrait of Elvire?

L.

Well, and if so succeed hand-practice on awry
Preposterous art-mistake, shall soul-proficiency
Despair, — when exercised on nature, which at worst
Always implies success, — however crossed and curst

By failure, — such as art would emulate in vain?
Shall any soul despair of setting free again
Trait after trait, until the type as wholly start
Forth, visible to sense, as that minutest part,
(Whate'er the chance,) which, first arresting eye, warned soul,
That, under wrong enough and ravage, lay the whole
O' the loveliness it "loved," — I take the accepted phrase?

LI.

So I account for tastes: each chooses, none gainsays
The fancy of his fellow, a paradise for him,
A hell for all beside. You can but crown the brim
O' the cup: if it be full, what matters less or more?
Let each i' the world amend his love, as I o' the shore
My sketch, and the result as undisputed be!
Their handiwork to them, and my Elvire to me:
Result more beautiful than Beauty's self, when, lo,
What was my Raphael turns my Michelagnolo!

LII.

For we two boast, beside our pearl, a diamond.
I' the palace-gallery, the corridor beyond,
Upheaves itself a marble, a magnitude man-shaped
As snow might be. One hand — the Master's — smoothed and scraped
That mass he hammered on and hewed at, till he hurled
Life out of death, and left a challenge: for the world,
Death still; since who shall dare, close to the image, say
If this be purposed Art, or mere mimetic play
Of Nature? — wont to deal with crag or cloud, as stuff
To fashion novel forms, like forms we know, enough
For recognition, but enough unlike the same
To leave no hope ourselves may profit by her game:
Death therefore to the world. Step back a pace or two!
And then who dares dispute the gradual birth its due
Of breathing life, or breathless immortality,
Where out she stands, and yet stops short, half bold, half shy,

Hesitates on the threshold of things, since partly blent
With stuff she needs must quit, her native element
I' the mind o' the Master, — what's the creature, dear-divine
Yet earthly-awful too, so manly-feminine,
Pretends this white advance? What startling brain-escape
Of Michelagnolo takes elemental shape?
I think he meant the daughter of the old man o' the sea,
Emerging from her wave, goddess Eidotheé, —
She who, in elvish sport, spite with benevolence
Mixed Mab-wise up, must needs instruct the hero whence
Salvation dawns o'er that mad misery of his isle.
Yes, she imparts to him by what a pranksome wile
He may surprise her sire, asleep beneath a rock,
When he has told their tale, amid his web-foot flock
Of sea-beasts, "fine fat seals with bitter breath!" laughs she
At whom she likes to save, no less: Eidotheé,

Whom you shall never face evolved, in earth, in air,
In wave; but, manifest i' the soul's domain,—why, there
She ravishingly moves to meet you, all through aid
O' the soul! Bid shine what should, dismiss into the shade
What should not be, and there triumphs the paramount
Emprise o' the Master! But attempt to make account
Of what the sense without the soul perceives? I bought
That work (despite plain proof whose hand it was had wrought
I' the rough, I think we trace the tool of triple-tooth
Here, there, and everywhere),—bought dearly that uncouth,
Unwieldy bulk, for just ten dollars,—"Bulk would fetch—
Converted into lime—some five pauls!" grinned a wretch,
Who, bound on business, paused to hear the bargaining,
And would have pitied me "but for the fun o' the thing!"

LIII.

Shall such a wretch be — you? Must — while I show Elvire
Shaming all other forms, seen as I see her here
I' the soul — this other-you perversely look outside,
And ask me, "Where i' the world is charm to be descried
I' the tall thin personage, with paled eye, pensive face,
Any amount of love, and some remains of grace?"
See yourself in my soul!

LIV.

And what a world for each
Must somehow be i' the soul! — accept that mode of speech, —
Whether an *aura* gird the soul, wherein it seems
To float and move, a belt of all the glints and gleams
It struck from out that world its weaklier fellows found
So dead and cold; or whether these not so much surround
As pass into the soul itself, add worth to worth,
As wine enriches blood, and straightway send it forth,

Conquering and to conquer, through all eternity:
That's battle without end.

LV.

I search but cannot see
What purpose serves the soul that strives, or world it tries
Conclusions with, unless the fruit of victories
Stay, one and all, stored up and guaranteed its own
Forever by some mode whereby shall be made known
The gain of every life. Death reads the title clear, —
What each soul for itself conquered from out things here;
Since in the seeing soul all worth lies, I assert,
And nought i' the world, which, save for soul that sees, inert
Was, is, and would be ever, — stuff for transmuting, — null
And void until man's breath evoke the beautiful;
But, touched aright, prompt yields each particle its tongue
Of elemental flame, no matter whence flame sprung

From gums and spice, or else from straw and rotten-
    ness,
So long as soul has power to make them burn, express
What lights and warms henceforth, leaves only ash
    behind,
Howe'er the chance: if soul be privileged to find
Food so soon, that at first snatch of eye, suck of breath,
It shall absorb pure life; or, rather, meeting death
I' the shape of ugliness, by fortunate recoil
So put on its resource, it finds therein a foil
For a new birth of life, the challenged soul's response
To ugliness and death, — creation for the nonce.

LVI.

I gather heart through just such conquests of the soul,
Through evocation out of that, which, on the whole,
Was rough, ungainly, partial accomplishment at best,
And — what, at worst, save failure to spit at and
    detest? —
Through transference of all, achieved in visible things,
To rest, secure from wrong, 'mid mere imaginings;

Through ardor to bring help just where completion halts,
Do justice to the purpose, ignore the slips and faults;
And last, not least, with stark deformity through fight
Which wrings thence, at the end, precise its opposite.
I praise the loyalty o' the scholar — stung by taunt
Of fools, "Does this evince thy Master they so vaunt?
Did he then perpetrate the plain abortion here?" —
Who cries, "His work am I! full fraught by him, I clear
His fame from each result of accident and time,
And thus restore his work to its fresh morning-prime:
Not daring touch the mass of marble, fools deride,
But putting my idea in plaster by its side,
His, since mine; I, he made, vindicate who made me!"

LVII.

For, you must know, I too achieve Eidotheé,
In silence and by night, — dared justify the lines
Plain to my soul, although, to sense, that triple-tine's
Achievement halt half-way, break down, or leave a blank.
If she stood forth at last, the Master was to thank!

Yet may there not have smiled approval in his eyes, —
That one at least was left, who, born to recognize
Perfection in the piece imperfect, worked that night
In silence, such his faith, until the apposite
Design was out of him, truth palpable once more;
And then — for at one blow its fragments strewed the floor —
Recalled the same to live within his soul as heretofore.

LVIII.

And, even as I hold and have Eidotheé,
I say, I cannot think that gains, — which would not be
Except a special soul had gained them, — that such gain
Can ever be estranged, do aught but appertain
Immortally, by right firm, indefeasible,
To who performed the feat, through God's grace and man's will!
Gain never shared by those who practised with earth's stuff,
And spoiled whate'er they touch, leaving its roughness rough,

Its blankness bare, and, when the ugliness opposed,
Either struck work, or laughed, "He doted or he dozed!"

LIX.

While, oh, how all the more will love become intense
Hereafter, when "to love" means yearning to dispense,
Each soul, its own amount of gain, through its own mode
Of practising with life, upon some soul which owed
Its treasure, all diverse, and yet in worth the same,
To new work and changed way! Things furnish you rose-flame,
Which burn up red, green, blue, nay, yellow, more than needs,
For me, I nowise doubt: why doubt a time succeeds
When each one may impart, and each receive, both share
The chemic secret, learn, where I lit force,—why, there
You drew forth lambent pity; where I found only food
For self-indulgence, you still blew a spark at brood
I' the grayest ember, stopped not till self-sacrifice imbued

Heaven's face with flame? What joy when each may supplement
The other, changing each, as changed, till, wholly blent,
The old things shall be new, and, what we both ignite,
Fuse, lose the varicolor in achromatic white!
Exemplifying law, apparent even now
In the eternal progress, — love's law, which I avow,
And thus would formulate: each soul lives, longs, and works
For itself, by itself, because a loadstar lurks,
An other than itself, — in whatsoe'er the niche
Of mistiest heaven it hide, whoe'er the Glumdalclich
May grasp the Gulliver: or it, or he, or she, —
Theosutós e broteios eper kekramene, —
(For fun's sake, where the phrase has fastened, leave it fixed!
So soft it says, — God, man, or both together mixed!)
This, guessed at through the flesh, by parts which prove the whole,
This constitutes the soul discernible by soul, —
Elvire, by me!

LX.

"And then" (so you permit remain
This hand upon my arm! — your cheek dried, if you deign,
Choosing my shoulder) — "then!" (stand up for, boldly state,
The objection in its length and breadth!) — "you abdicate,
With boast yet on your lip, soul's empire, and accept
The rule of sense; the man, from monarch's throne has stept, —
Leaped, rather, at one bound, to base, and there lies, brute.
You talk of soul, — how soul, in search of soul to suit,
Must needs review the sex, the army rank and file
Of womankind; report no face nor form so vile
But that a certain worth, by certain signs, may thence
Evolve itself, and stand confessed — to soul — by sense.
Sense? Oh, the loyal bee endeavors for the hive!
Disinterested hunts the flower-field through, alive

Not one mean moment, no, — suppose on flower he light, —
To his peculiar drop, petal-dew perquisite,
Matter-of-course snatched snack: unless he taste, how try?
This, light on tongue-tip laid, allows him pack his thigh,
Transport all he counts prize, provision for the comb,
Food for the future day, — a banquet, but at home!
Soul? Ere you reach Fifine's, some flesh may be to pass!
That bombèd brow, that eye, a kindling chrysoprase,
Beneath its stiff black lash, inquisitive how speeds
Each functionary limb, how play of foot succeeds,
And how you let escape or duly sympathize
With gastro-knemian grace, — true, your soul tastes and tries,
And trifles time with these, but, fear not, will arrive
At essence in the core, bring honey home to hive,
Brain-stock and heart-stuff both, — to strike objectors dumb, —
Since only soul affords the soul fit pabulum!

Be frank for charity! Who is it you deceive —
Yourself or me or God — with all this make-believe?"

LXI.

And frank I will respond as you interrogate.
Ah, Music, wouldst thou help! Words struggle with the weight
So feebly of the False, thick element between
Our soul, the True, and Truth! which, but that intervene
False shows of things, were reached as easily by thought
Reducible to word, as now by yearnings wrought
Up with thy fine, free force, O Music! that canst thrid,
Electrically win, a passage through the lid
Of earthly sepulchre, our words may push against,
Hardly transpierce as thou! Not dissipate, thou deign'st,
So much as tricksily elude what words attempt
To heave away, i' the mass, and let the soul, exempt
From all that vapory obstruction, view, instead
Of glimmer underneath, a glory overhead.

Not feebly, like our phrase, against the barrier go
In suspirative swell the authentic notes I know;
By help whereof, I would our souls were found without
The pale, above the dense and dim which breeds the
doubt!
But Music, dumb for you, withdraws her help from me;
And, since to weary words recourse again must be,
At least permit they rest their burthen here and there,
Music-like: cover space! My answer — need you care
If it exceed the bounds, reply to questioning
You never meant should plague? Once fairly on the
wing,
Let me flap far and wide!

LXII.

For this is just the time,
The place, the mood in you and me, when all things
chime,
Clash forth life's common chord; whence, list how there
ascend
Harmonics far and faint, till our perception end, —

Reverberated notes whence we construct the scale
Embracing what we know and feel and are! How fail
To find, or, better, lose your question, in this quick
Reply which Nature yields, ample and catholic?
For, arm in arm, we two have reached, nay, passed, you see,
The village-precinct: sun sets mild on Saint-Marie,—
We only catch the spire; and yet I seem to know
What's hid i' the turn o' the hill; how all the graves must glow
Soberly, as each warms its little iron cross,
Flourished about with gold, and graced (if private loss
Be fresh) with stiff rope-wreath of yellow, crisp bead-blooms
Which tempt down birds to pay their supper, 'mid the tombs,
With prattle good as song, amuse the dead a while,
If couched they hear beneath the matted camomile!

LXIII.

Bid them good-by before last friend has sung and supped!
Because we pick our path, and need our eyes, — abrupt
Descent enough; but here's the beach, and there's the bay,
And, opposite, the streak of Isle Noirmoutier.
Thither the waters tend: they freshen as they haste,
At feel o' the night-wind; though, by cliff and cliff embraced,
This breadth of blue retains its self-possession still;
As you and I intend to do, who take our fill
Of sights and sounds, — soft sound, the countless hum and skip
Of insects we disturb, and that good fellowship
Of rabbits our foot-fall sends huddling, each to hide
He best knows how and where; and what whirred past, wings wide?
That was an owl, their young may justlier apprehend!
Though you refuse to speak, your beating heart, my friend,

I feel against my arm; though your bent head forbids
A look into your eyes, yet on my cheek their lids,
That ope and shut, soft send a silken thrill the same.
Well, out of all and each these nothings comes — what
came
Often enough before — the something that would aim
Once more at the old mark; the impulse to at last
Succeed where hitherto was failure in the past,
And yet again essay the adventure. Clearlier sings
No bird to its couched corpse, "Into the truth of things —
Out of their falseness rise, and reach thou, and remain!"

LXIV.

"That rise into the true out of the false — explain?"
May an example serve? In yonder bay I bathed
This sunny morning; swam my best; then hung, half
swathed
With chill and half with warmth, i' the channel's mid-
most deep:
You know how one — not treads, but stands in water?
Keep

Body and limbs below, hold head back, uplift chin,
And, for the rest, leave care! If brow, eyes, mouth, should win
Their freedom, — excellent! If they must brook the surge,
No matter though they sink, let but the nose emerge.
So all of me in brine lay soaking: did I care
One jot? I kept alive by man's due breath of air
I' the nostrils, high and dry. At times, o'er these would run
The ripple, even wash the wavelet; for the sun
Tempted advance, no doubt: and always flash of froth,
Fish-outbreak, bubbling by, would find me nothing loath
To rise and look around; then all was overswept
With dark and death at once. But trust the old adept!
Back went again the head; a merest motion made,
Fin-fashion, either hand; and nostril soon conveyed
The news that light and life were still in reach as erst:
Always the last, and — wait and watch — sometimes the first.

Try to ascend breast-high? wave arms wide free of
tether?
Be in the air, and leave the water altogether?
Under went all again, till I resigned myself
To only breathe the air, that's footed by an elf;
And only swim the water, that's native to a fish.
But there is no denying, that ere I curbed my wish,
And schooled my restive arms, salt entered mouth and
eyes
Often enough, — sun, sky, and air so tantalize!
Still the adept swims, this accorded, that denied;
Can always breathe, sometimes see and be satisfied!

LXV.

I liken to this play o' the body — fruitless strife
To slip the sea, and hold the heaven — my spirit's life
'Twixt false, whence it would break, and true, where it
would bide.
I move in, yet resist; am upborne every side
By what I beat against, — an element too gross
To live in, did not soul duly obtain her dose

Of life-breath, and inhale from truth's pure plenitude
Above her, snatch and gain enough to just illude
With hope that some brave bound may baffle evermore
The obstructing medium, make who swam henceforward soar:
Gain scarcely snatched, when, foiled by the very effort, sowse,
Underneath ducks the soul, her truthward yearnings dowse
Deeper in falsehood! ay, but fitted less and less
To bear in nose and mouth old briny bitterness
Proved alien more and more; since each experience proves
Air the essential good, not sea, wherein who moves
Must thence, in the act, escape, apart from will or wish.
Move a mere hand to take waterweed, jelly-fish,
Upward you tend! And yet our business with the sea
Is not with air, but just o' the water, watery:
We must endure the false, no particle of which
Do we acquaint us with, but up we mount a pitch

Above it, find our head reach truth, while hands explore
The false below: so much while here we bathe, — no more!

LXVI.

Now, there is one prime point, (hear and be edified!)
One truth more true for me than any truth beside;
To wit, that I am I, who have the power to swim,
The skill to understand the law whereby each limb
May bear to keep immersed, since, in return, made sure
That its mere movement lifts head clean through coverture.
By practice with the false, I reach the true? Why, thence
It follows, that the more I gain self-confidence,
Get proof I know the trick, can float, sink, rise, at will,
The better I submit to what I have the skill
To conquer in my turn, even now, and by and by
Leave wholly for the land, and there laugh, shake me dry
To last drop, saturate with noonday, — no need more
Of wet and fret, plagued once: on Pornic's placid shore

Abundant air to breathe, sufficient sun to feel!
Meantime I buoy myself: no whit my senses reel
When over me there breaks a billow; nor, elate
Too much by some brief taste, I quaff intemperate
The air, o'ertop breast-high the wave-environment.
Full well I know, the thing I grasp, as if intent
To hold, — my wandering wave, — will not be grasped
  at all:
The solid-seeming grasped, the handful great or small
Must go to nothing, glide through fingers fast enough;
But none the less, to treat liquidity as stuff —
Though failure — certainly succeeds beyond its aim;
Sends head above, far past the thing hands miss, the
  same.

LXVII.

So with this wash o' the world, wherein life-long we
  drift:
We push and paddle through the foam by making shift
To breathe above at whiles, when, after deepest duck
Down underneath the show, we put forth hand, and pluck

At what seems somehow like reality,—a soul.
I catch at this and that to capture and control;
Presume I hold a prize; discover that my pains
Are run to nought; my hands are balked; my head regains
The surface, where I breathe and look about a space.
The soul that helped me mount? Swallowed up in the race
O' the tide, come who knows whence, gone gayly who knows where!
I thought the prize was mine; I flattered myself there.
It did its duty, though: I felt it; it felt me;
Or where I look about and breathe I should not be.
The main point is, the false fluidity was bound
Acknowledge that it frothed o'er substance nowise found
Fluid, but firm and true. Man, outcast, "howls,"—at rods?—
If "sent in playful spray a-shivering to his gods!"
Childishest childe, man makes thereby no bad exchange.
Stay with the flat-fish, thou! We like the upper range

Where the "gods" live, perchance the demons also dwell,
Where operates a Power, which every throb and swell
Of human heart invites that human soul approach,
"Sent" near and nearer still, however "spray" encroach
On "shivering" flesh below, to altitudes, which gained,
Evil proves good, wrong right, obscurity explained,
And "howling" childishness. Whose howl have we to thank
If all the dogs 'gan bark, and puppies whine, till sank
Each yelper's tail 'twixt legs? for Huntsman Common-sense
Came to the rescue; caused prompt thwack of thong dispense
Quiet i' the kennel; taught that ocean might be blue,
And rolling, and much more, and yet the soul have, too,
Its touch of God's own flame, which he may so expand
"Who measurèd the waters i' the hollow of his hand,"
That ocean's self shall dry, turn dew-drop in respect
Of all-triumphant fire, matter with intellect

Once fairly matched; bade him who egged on hounds to bay
Go curse i' the poultry-yard his kind: "there let him lay"
The swan's one addled egg; which yet shall put to use,
Rub breast-bone warm against, so many a sterile goose!

LXVIII.

No, I want sky, not sea; prefer the larks to shrimps;
And never dive so deep but that I get a glimpse
O' the blue above, a breath of the air around. Elvire,
I seize — by catching at that melted beryl here,
The tawny wavelet just has trickled off — Fifine!
Did not we two trip forth to just enjoy the scene, —
The tumbling-troop arrayed, the strollers on their stage
Drawn up and under arms, and ready to engage;
Dabble, and there an end, with foam and froth o'er face,
Till suddenly Fifine suggested change of place?
Now we taste ether, scorn the wave, and interchange apace

No ordinary thoughts, but such as evidence
The cultivated mind in both! On what pretence
Are you and I to sneer at who lent help to hand,
And gave the lucky lift?

LXIX.

Still sour? I understand!
One ugly circumstance discredits my fair plan,—
That woman does the work: I waive the help of man.
"Why should experiment be tried with only waves,
When solid spars float round? Still some Thalassia saves
Too pertinaciously, as though no Triton, bluff
As e'er blew brine from conch, were free to help enough!
Surely, to recognize a man, his mates serve best!
Why is there not the same or greater interest
In the strong spouse as in the pretty partner, pray?
Were recognition just your object, as you say,
Amid this element o' the false."

LXX.

We come to terms.
I need to be proved true; and nothing so confirms
One's faith in the prime point that one's alive, not dead,
In all descents to hell whereof I ever read,
As when a phantom there, male enemy or friend,
Or merely stranger-shade, is struck, is forced suspend
His passage: "You that breathe, along with us the ghosts?"
Here why must it still be a woman that accosts?

LXXI.

Because one woman's worth, in that respect, such hairy hosts
Of the other sex and sort! Men? Say you have the power
To make them yours, rule men, throughout life's little hour,
According to the phrase; what follows? Men you make,
By ruling them, your own: each man for his own sake

Accepts you as his guide, avails him of what worth
He apprehends in you to sublimate his earth
With fire; content, if so you convoy him through night,
That you shall play the sun, and he, the satellite,
Pilfer your light and heat and virtue, starry pelf,
While, caught up by your course, he turns upon himself.
Women rush into you, and there remain absorbed.
Beside, 'tis only men completely formed, full-orbed,
Are fit to follow track, keep pace, illustrate so
The leader: any sort of woman may bestow
Her atom on the star, or clod she counts for such;
Each little making less bigger by just that much.
Women grow you, while men depend on you at best.
And what dependence! Bring and put him to the test,
Your specimen disciple, a handbreadth separate
From you, he almost seemed to touch before! Abate
Complacency you will, I judge, at what's divulged!
Some flabbiness you fixed, some vacancy out-bulged,

Some, — much, — nay, all, perhaps, the outward man's
your work;
But inside man? — find him, wherever he may lurk,
And where's a touch of you in his true self?

LXXII.

I wish
Some wind would waft this way a glassy bubble-fish
O' the kind the sea inflates, and show you, once detached
From wave — or no; the event is better told than watched:
Still may the thing float free, globose and opaline
All over, save where just the amethysts combine
To blue their best, rim-round the sea-flower with a tinge
Earth's violet never knew! Well, 'neath that gem-tipped fringe
A head lurks — of a kind — that acts as stomach too;
Then comes the emptiness which out the water blew
So big and belly-like, but, dry of water drained,
Withers away nine-tenths. Ah, but a tenth remained!

That was the creature's self; no more akin to sea,
Poor rudimental head and stomach, you agree,
Than sea's akin to who dips yonder his red edge.

LXXIII.

But take the rillet, ends a race o'er yonder ledge
O' the fissured cliff, to find its fate in smoke below!
Disengage that, and ask — what news of life, you know
It led, that long lone way, through pasture, plain, and
waste?
All's gone to give the sea! no touch of earth, no taste
Of air, reserved to tell how rushes used to bring
The butterfly and bee, and fisher-bird that's king
O' the purple kind, about the snow-soft, silver-sweet
Infant of mist and dew; only these atoms fleet,
Imbittered evermore, to make the sea one drop
More big thereby, — if thought keep count where sense
must stop.

LXXIV.

The full-blown ingrate, mere recipient of the brine,
That takes all, and gives nought, is man: the feminine

Rillet, that taking all, and giving nought in turn,
Goes headlong to her death i' the sea, without concern
For the old inland life, snow-soft and silver-clear,—
That's woman, typified from Fifine to Elvire.

LXXV.

Then how diverse the modes prescribed to who would deal
With either kind of creature! 'Tis man you seek to seal
Your very own? Resolve, for first step, to discard
Nine-tenths of what you are! To make, you must be marred;
To raise your race, must stoop; to teach them aught, must learn
Ignorance, meet half way what most you hope to spurn
I' the sequel. Change yourself, dissimulate the thought
And vulgarize the word, and see the deed be brought
To look like nothing done with any such intent
As teach men,—though perchance it teach by accident!
So may you master men; assured that if you show
One point of mastery, departure from the low

And level, — head or heart revolt at long disguise,
Immurement, stifling soul in mediocrities, —
If inadvertently a gesture, much more, word,
Reveal the hunter no companion for the herd,
His chance of capture's gone. Success means, they may snuff,
Examine, and report, — a brother, sure enough,
Disports him in brute-guise; for skin is truly skin,
Horns, hoofs, are hoofs and horns, and all, outside and in,
Is veritable beast, whom fellow-beasts resigned
May follow, made a prize in honest pride, behind
One of themselves, and not creation's upstart lord!
Well, there's your prize i' the pound: much joy may it afford
My Indian! Make survey, and tell me, — was it worth
You acted part so well, went all-fours upon on earth
The live-long day, brayed, belled, and all to bring to pass
That stags should deign eat hay when winter stints them grass?

LXXVI.

So much for men, and how disguise may make them mind
Their master. But you have to deal with womankind?
Abandon stratagem for strategy; cast quite
The vile disguise away; try truth clean-opposite
Such creep-and-crawl; stand forth all man, and, might it chance,
Somewhat of angel too! — whate'er inheritance,
Actual on earth, in heaven prospective, be your boast,
Lay claim to! Your best self revealed at uttermost —
That's the wise way o' the strong! And, e'en should falsehood tempt
The weaker sort to swerve, at least the lie's exempt
From slur, that's loathlier still, of aiming to debase
Rather than elevate its object. Mimic grace,
Not make deformity your mask! Be sick by stealth,
Nor traffic with disease, — malingering in health!
No more of — "Countrymen, I boast me one like you, —
My lot, the common strength, the common weakness too!

I think the thoughts you think; and if I have the knack
Of fitting thoughts to words, you peradventure lack,
Envy me not the chance, yourselves more fortunate!
Many the loaded ship self-sunk through treasure-freight;
Many the pregnant brain brings never child to birth;
Many the great heart bursts beneath its girdle-girth!
Be mine the privilege to supplement defect,
Give dumbness voice, and let the laboring intellect
Find utterance in word, or possibly in deed!
What though I seem to go before? 'tis you that lead!
I follow what I see so plain, — the general mind
Projected pillar-wise, flame kindled by the kind,
Which dwarfs the unit — me — to insignificance!
Halt you, I stop forthwith; proceed, I too advance!"

LXXVII.

Ay, that's the way to take with men you wish to lead,
Instruct, and benefit. Small prospect you succeed
With women so! Be all that's great and good and wise,
August, sublime; swell out your frog the right ox-size:

He's buoyed like a balloon, to soar, not burst, you'll
see!
The more you prove yourself, less fear the prize will flee
The captor. Here you start after no pompous stag
Who condescends be snared, with toss of horn, and brag
Of bray, and ramp of hoof; you have not to subdue
The foe through letting him imagine he snares you:
'Tis rather with —

LXXVIII.

Ah, thanks! quick! — where the
dipping disk
Shows red against the rise and fall o' the fin! there frisk
In shoal the — porpoises? Dolphins, they shall and
must
Cut through the freshening clear; dolphins, my in-
stance just!
'Tis fable, therefore truth: who has to do with these
Needs never practise trick of going hands and knees
As beasts require. Art fain the fish to captivate?
Gather thy greatness round, Arion! Stand in state,

As when the banqueting thrilled conscious,—like a rose
Throughout its hundred leaves at that approach it knows
Of music in the bird,—while Corinth grew one breast
A-throb for song and thee; nay, Periander pressed
The Methymnæan hand, and felt a king indeed, and guessed
How Phœbus' self might give that great mouth of the gods
Such a magnificence of song! The pillar nods,
Rocks roof, and trembles door, gigantic, post and jamb,
As harp and voice rend air,—the shattering dithyramb!
So stand thou, and assume the robe that tingles yet
With triumph; strike the harp, whose every golden fret
Still smoulders with the flame was late at finger's end:
So, standing on the bench o' the ship, let voice expend
Thy soul; sing, unalloyed by meaner mode, thine own,
The Orthian lay; then leap from Music's lofty throne
Into the lowest surge, make fearlessly thy launch!
Whatever storm may threat, some dolphin will be stanch!

Whatever roughness rage, some exquisite sea-thing
Will surely rise to save, will bear — palpitating —
One proud humility of love beneath its load,
Stem tide, part wave, till both roll on, thy jewelled road
Of triumph, and the grim o' the gulf grow wonder-
white
I' the phosphorescent wake; and still the exquisite
Sea-thing stems on, saves still, palpitatingly thus,
Lands safe at length its love of load at Tænarus,
True woman-creature!

LXXIX.

Man? Ah! would you prove what power
Marks man; what fruit his tree may yield beyond the
sour
And stinted crab he calls love-apple, which remains
After you toil and moil your utmost, — all, love gains
By lavishing manure? — try quite the other plan!
And, to obtain the strong true product of a man,
Set him to hate a little! Leave cherishing his root,
And rather prune his branch, nip off the pettiest shoot

Superfluous on his bough! I promise, you shall learn
By what grace came the goat, of all beasts else, to earn
Such favor with the god o' the grape: 'twas only he
Who, browsing on its tops, first stung fertility
Into the stock's heart, stayed much growth of tendril-twine,
Some faintish flower, perhaps, but gained the indignant wine,
Wrath of the red press! Catch the puniest of the kind, —
Man-animalcule, starved body, stunted mind, —
And, as you nip the blotch 'twixt thumb and finger-nail,
Admire how heaven above and earth below avail
No jot to soothe the mite, sore at God's prime offence
In making mites at all; coax from its impotence
One virile drop of thought or word or deed, by strain
To propagate for once, — which nature rendered vain,
Who lets first failure stay, yet cares not to record
Mistake that seems to cast opprobrium on the Lord!

Such were the gain from love's best pains! But let the elf
Be touched with hate because some real man bears himself
Manlike in body and soul, and, since he lives, must thwart
And furify and set a-fizz this counterpart
O' the pismire that's surprised to effervescence, if,
By chance, black bottle come in contact with chalk cliff,
Acid with alkali! Then thrice the bulk, out blows
Our insect, does its kind, and cuckoo-spits some rose!

LXXX.

No: 'tis ungainly work, the ruling men, at best!
The graceful instinct's right: 'tis women stand confessed
Auxiliary, the gain that never goes away,
Takes nothing, and gives all: Elvire, Fifine, 'tis they
Convince, — if little, much, no matter! — one degree
The more, at least, convince unreasonable me

That I am, anyhow, a truth, though all else seem
And be not: if I dream, at least I know I dream.
The falsity, beside, is fleeting: I can stand
Still, and let truth come back, — your steadying touch of hand
Assists me to remain self-centred, fixed amid
All on the move. Believe in me, at once you bid
Myself believe, that, since one soul has disengaged
Mine from the shows of things, so much is fact: I waged
No foolish warfare, then, with shades, myself a shade,
Here in the world; may hope my pains will be repaid!
How false things are, I judge; how changeable, I learn:
When, where, and how it is I shall see truth return,
That I expect to know, because Fifine knows me!
How much more, if Elvire!

LXXXI.

"And why not, only she?
Since there can be for each one Best, no more, such Best,
For body and mind of him, abolishes the rest

O' the simply Good and Better. You please select Elvire
To give you this belief in truth; dispel the fear
Yourself are, after all, as false as what surrounds;
And why not be content? When we two watched the rounds
The boatman made 'twixt shoal and sandbank yesterday,
As, at dead slack of tide, he chose to push his way
With oar and pole across the creek, and reach the isle
After a world of pains, my word provoked your smile,
Yet none the less deserved reply: ''Twere wiser wait
The turn o' the tide, and find conveyance for his freight —
How easily — within the ship to purpose moored,
Managed by sails, not oars! But no: the man's allured
By liking for the new and hard in his exploit!
First come shall serve! He makes — courageous and adroit —
The merest willow-leaf of boat do duty, bear
His merchandise across: once over, needs he care

If folk arrive by ship six hours hence, fresh and gay?'
No: he scorns commonplace; affects the unusual way;
And good Elvire is moored, with not a breath to flap
The yards of her; no lift of ripple to o'erlap
Keel, much less prow. What care? since here's a cockle-shell,
Fifine, that's taut and crank, and carries just as well
Such seamanship as yours!"

LXXXII.

Alack, our life is lent,
From first to last, the whole, for this experiment
Of proving what I say, — that we ourselves are true!
I would there were one voyage, and then no more to do
But tread the firm land, tempt the uncertain sea no more!
I would we might dispense with change of shore for shore
To evidence our skill, demonstrate — in no dream
It was we tided o'er the trouble of the stream!
I would the steady voyage, and not the fitful trip, —
Elvire, and not Fifine, — might test our seamanship!

But why expend one's breath to tell you change of boat
Means change of tactics too? Come see the same afloat
To-morrow, all the change, new stowage fore and aft
O' the cargo; then to cross requires new sailor-craft!
To-day one step from stern to bow keeps boat in trim:
To-morrow some big stone — or woe to boat and him! —
Must ballast both. That man stands for Mind, paramount
Throughout the adventure: ay, howe'er you make account,
'Tis mind that navigates; skips over, twists between
The bales i' the boat; now gives importance to the mean,
And now abates the pride of life, accepts all fact,
Discards all fiction; steers Fifine, and cries, in the act,
"Thou art so bad, and yet so delicate a brown!
Wouldst tell no end of lies: I talk to smile or frown!
Wouldst rob me: do men blame a squirrel, lithe and sly,
For pilfering the nut she adds to hoard? Nor I.

Elvire is true as truth, honesty's self, alack!
The worse! too safe the ship, the transport there and back
Too certain! one may loll and lounge and leave the helm,
Let wind and tide do work: no fear that waves o'erwhelm
The steady-going bark, as sure to feel her way
Blind-fold across, reach land, next year as yesterday!
How can I but suspect the true feat were to slip
Down side, transfer myself to cockle-shell from ship,
And try if, trusting to sea-tracklessness, I class
With those around whose breast grew oak and triple brass;
Who dreaded no degree of death, but with dry eyes
Surveyed the turgid main and its monstrosities,
And rendered futile, so, the prudent Power's decree
Of separate earth and disassociating sea?
Since how is it observed, if impious vessels leap
Across, and tempt a thing they should not touch, — the deep?

(See Horace to the boat, wherein, for Athens bound,
When Virgil must embark — Jove keep him safe and
sound! —
The poet bade his friend start on the watery road,
Much re-assured by this so comfortable ode.")

LXXXIII.

Then never grudge my poor Fifine her compliment!
The rakish craft could slip her moorings in the tent,
And, hoisting every stitch of spangled canvas, steer
Through divers rocks and shoals; in fine, deposit here
Your Virgil of a spouse in Attica; yea, thrid
The mob of men, select the special virtue hid
In him, forsooth, and say, or rather smile so sweet,
"Of all the multitude, you — I prefer to cheat!
Are you for Athens bound? I can perform the trip,
Shove little pinnace off, while yon superior ship,
The Elvire, refits in port!" So off we push from beach
Of Pornic Town: and lo, ere eye can wink, we reach
The Long Walls, and I prove that Athens is no dream;
For there the temples rise! they are; they nowise seem!

Earth is not all one lie, this truth attests me true!
Thanks, therefore, to Fifine! Elvire, I'm back with you!
Share in the memories! Embark I trust we shall
Together some fine day, and so, for good and all,
Bid Pornic Town adieu; then just the strait to cross,
And we reach harbor, safe, in Iostephanos!

LXXXIV.

How quickly night comes! Lo! already 'tis the land
Turns sea-like: overcrept by gray, the plains expand,
Assume significance; while ocean dwindles, shrinks
Into a pettier bound: its plash and plaint, methinks,
Six steps away, how both retire, as if their part
Were played, another force were free to prove her art,
Protagonist in turn! Are you unterrified?
All false, all fleeting too! And nowhere things abide,
And everywhere we strain that things should stay, — the one
Truth, that ourselves are true!

LXXXV.

A word, and I have done.
Is it not just our hate of falsehood, fleetingness,
And the mere part things play, that constitutes express
The inmost charm of this Fifine and all her tribe?
Actors! We also act; but only they inscribe
Their style and title so, and preface — only they —
Performance with, "A lie is all we do or say."
Wherein but there can be the attraction, Falsehood's bribe,
That wins so surely o'er to Fifine and her tribe
The liking, nay, the love, of who hate Falsehood most,
Except that these alone of mankind make their boast,
"Frankly, we simulate!" To feign means — to have grace,
And so get gratitude! This ruler of the race,
Crowned, sceptred, stoled to suit, — 'tis not that you detect
The cobbler in the king, but that he makes effect
By seeming the reverse of what you know to be
The man, the mind, whole form, fashion, and quality.

Mistake his false for true one minute, — there's an end
Of the admiration! Truth we grieve at or rejoice:
'Tis only falsehood, plain in gesture, look, and voice,
That brings the praise desired, since profit comes thereby.
The histrionic truth is in the natural lie.
Because the man who wept the tears was, all the time,
Happy enough; because the other man, a-grime
With guilt, was, at the least, as white as I and you;
Because the timid type of bashful maidhood, who
Starts at her own pure shade, already numbers seven
Born babes, and in a month will turn their odd to even;
Because the saucy prince would prove, could you unfurl
Some yards of wrap, a meek and meritorious girl, —
Precisely as you see success attained by each
O' the mimes, do you approve, not foolishly impeach
The falsehood!

LXXXVI.

That's the first o' the truths found: all things, slow
Or quick i' the passage, come at last to that, you know!

Each has a false outside, whereby a truth is forced
To issue from within: truth, falsehood, are divorced
By the excepted eye, at the rare season, for
The happy moment. Life means — learning to abhor
The false, and love the true, — truth treasured snatch by snatch,
Waifs counted at their worth. And when with strays they match
I' the party-colored world; when under foul shines fair,
And truth, displayed i' the point, flashes forth everywhere
I' the circle, manifest to soul, though hid from sense,
And no obstruction more affects this confidence;
When faith is ripe for sight, — why, reasonably, then
Comes the great clearing-up. Wait threescore years and ten!

LXXXVII.

Therefore I prize stage-play, the honest cheating; thence
The impulse pricked, when fife and drum bade Fair commence,

To bid you trip and skip, link arm in arm with me,
Like husband and like wife, and so together see
The tumbling-troop arrayed, the strollers on their stage
Drawn up and under arms, and ready to engage.
And if I started thence upon abstruser themes—
Well, 'twas a dream, pricked too!

LXXXVIII.

A poet never dreams:
We prose-folk always do: we miss the proper duct
For thoughts on things unseen, which stagnate and obstruct
The system, therefore: mind, sound in a body sane,
Keeps thoughts apart from facts, and to one flowing vein
Confines its sense of that which is not, but might be,
And leaves the rest alone. What ghosts do poets see?
What demons fear? what man or thing misapprehend?
Unchoked, the channel's flush, the fancy's free to spend
Its special self aright in manner, time, and place.
Never believe that who create the busy race

O' the brain, bring poetry to birth, such act performed,
Feel trouble them, the same, such residue as warmed
My prosy blood this morn, — intrusive fancies, meant
For outbreak and escape by quite another vent!
Whence follows, that, asleep, my dreamings oft exceed
The bound. But you shall hear.

LXXXIX.

I smoked. The webs o' the weed,
With many a break i' the mesh, were floating to re-form
Cupola-wise above; chased thither by soft, warm
Inflow of air without; since I, — of mind to muse, to clench
The gain of soul and body got by their noon-day drench
In sun and sea, — I flung both frames o' the window wide,
To soak my body still, and let soul soar beside.
In came the country sounds and sights and smells, — that fine
Sharp needle in the nose from our fermenting wine!

In came a dragon-fly with whir and stir, then out,
Off, and away; in came — kept coming, rather, pout
Succeeding smile, and take-away still close on give —
One loose long creeper-branch, tremblingly sensitive
To risk, which blooms and leaves, — each leaf tongue-broad, each bloom
Mid-finger-deep, — must run by prying in the room
Of one who loves and grasps and spoils and speculates.
All, so far, plain enough to sight and sense: but weights,
Measures, and numbers, — ah! could one apply such test
To other visitants that came at no request
Of who kept open house; to fancies manifold
From this four-cornered world, the memories new and old,
The antenatal prime experience — what know I? —
The initiatory love preparing us to die, —
Such were a crowd to count, a sight to see, a prize
To turn to profit, were but fleshly ears and eyes
Able to cope with those o' the spirit!

XC.

Therefore, — since
Thought hankers after speech, while no speech may evince
Feeling like music, — mine, o'erburthened with each gift
From every visitant, at last resolved to shift
Its burthen to the back of some musician dead
And gone, who, feeling once what I feel now, instead
Of words, sought sounds, and saved forever, in the same,
Truth that escapes prose; nay, puts poetry to shame.
One reads the note, one strikes the key, one bids *record*
The instrument, — thanks for the veritable word!
And not in vain one cries, "O dead and gone away,
Assist who struggles yet, thy strength become my stay,
Thy record serve as well to register, — I felt
And knew thus much of truth! With me must knowledge melt
Into surmise and doubt and disbelief, unless
Thy music re-assure, — I gave no idle guess,
But gained a certitude myself may hardly keep!
What care? since round is piled a monumental heap

Of music that conserves the assurance thou as well
Wast certain of the same! — thou, master of the spell,
Mad'st moonbeams marble, didst *record* what other men
Feel only to forget!" Who was it helped me, then?
What master's work first came responsive to my call,
Found my eye, fixed my choice?

XCI.

Why, Schumann's "Carnival"!
Choice chiming in, you see, exactly with the sounds
And sights of yester-eve, when, going on my rounds,
Where both roads join the bridge, I heard across the dusk
Creak a slow caravan, and saw arrive the husk
O' the spice-nut, which peeled off this morning, and displayed
'Twixt tree and tree a tent whence the red pennon made
Its vivid reach for home and ocean-idleness,
And where, my heart surmised, at that same moment, — yes, —

Tugging her tricot on, yet tenderly, lest stitch
Announce the crack of doom, reveal disaster which
Our Pornic's modest stock of merceries in vain
Were ransacked to retrieve, — there, cautiously a-strain,
(My heart surmised) must crouch in that tent's corner, curved
Like spring-month's russet moon, some beauty fate reserved
To give me once again the electric snap and spark
That prove, when finger finds out finger in the dark
O' the world, there's fire and life and truth there, link but hands,
And pass the secret on! till, link by link, expands
The circle, lengthens out the chain; and one embrace
Of high with low is found uniting the whole race, —
Not simply you and me and our Fifine, but all
The world: the Fair expands into the Carnival,
And Carnival again to — Ah, but that's my dream!

XCII.

I somehow played the piece; remarked on each old theme

I' the new dress; saw how food o' the soul, the stuff
that's made
To furnish man with thought and feeling, is purveyed
Substantially the same from age to age, with change
Of the outside only for successive feasters. Range
The banquet-room o' the world, from the dim farthest
head
O' the table to its foot, for you and me bespread
This merry morn, we find sufficient fare, I trow.
But novel? Scrape away the sauce, and taste, below,
The verity o' the viand, you shall perceive there went
To board-head just the dish which other condiment
Makes palatable now: guests came, sat down, fell to,
Rose up, wiped mouth, went way, — lived, died, — and
never knew
That generations yet should, seeking sustenance,
Still find the selfsame fare, with somewhat to enhance
Its flavor in the kind of cooking. As with hates
And loves and fears and hopes, so with what emulates
The same, expresses hates, loves, fears, and hopes in art:
The forms, the themes, — no one without its counterpart

Ages ago; no one, but, mumbled the due time
I' the mouth of the eater, needs be cooked again in
rhyme,
Dished up anew in paint, sauce-smothered fresh in
sound,
To suit the wisdom-tooth, just cut, of the age, that's
found
With gums obtuse to gust and smack which relished so
The meat o' the meal folks made some fifty years ago.
But don't suppose the new was able to efface
The old without a struggle, a pang! The common-
place
Still clung about his heart long after all the rest
O' the natural man, at eye and ear, was caught, con-
fessed
The charm of change, although wry lip and wrinkled
nose
Owned ancient virtue more conducive to repose
Than modern nothing roused to something by some
shred
Of pungency, perchance garlic in amber's stead?

And so on, till, one day, another age, by due
Rotation, pries, sniffs, smacks, discovers old is new,
And sauce our sires pronounced insipid proves again
Sole piquant, and resumes its titillating reign,
With music, most of all the arts, since change is there
The law, and not the lapse: the precious means the rare,
And not the absolute in all good save surprise.
So I remarked upon our Schumann's victories
Over the commonplace, how faded phrase grew fine,
And palled perfection, piqued, upstartled by that brine,
His pickle, bit the mouth and burnt the tongue aright,
Beyond the merely good no longer exquisite;
Then took things as I found, and thanked without demur
The pretty piece, — played through that movement, you prefer,
Where dance and shuffle past, he scolding while she pouts,
She canting while he calms, in those eternal bouts
Of age, the dog — with youth, the cat — by rose-festoon
Tied teasingly forever, — Columbine, Pantaloon,

She, toe-tips and *staccato*, — *legato*, shakes his poll
And shambles in pursuit, the senior. *Fi la folle!*
Lie to him! get his gold, and pay its price! begin
Your trade betimes, nor wait till you've wed Harlequin,
And need, at the week's end, to play the duteous wife,
And swear you still love slaps and leapings more than life!
Pretty! I say.

XCIII.

And so I somehow-nohow played
The whole o' the pretty piece; and then — whatever weighed
My eyes down, furled the films about my wits, — suppose,
The morning-bath, — the sweet monotony of those
Three keys, flat, flat and flat, never a sharp at all;
Or else the brain's fatigue, forced even here to fall
Into the same old track, and recognize the shift
From old to new, and back to old again, and, swift
Or slow, no matter, still the certainty of change,
Conviction we shall find the false, where'er we range,

In art no less than nature,—or what if wrist were numb,
And over-tense the mucle, abductor of the thumb,
Taxed by those tenths' and twelfths' unconscionable stretch?
Howe'er it came to pass, I soon was far to fetch,—
Gone off in company with Music!

XCIV.

Whither bound
Except for Venice? She it was, by instinct found,
Carnival-country proper, who, far below the perch
Where I was pinnacled, showed, opposite, Mark's Church,
And, underneath, Mark's Square, with those two lines of street,
Procuratié-sides, each leading to my feet;
Since I gazed from above, however I got there.

XCV.

And what I gazed upon was a prodigious Fair,

Concourse immense of men and women, crowned or casqued,
Turbaned or tiar'd, wreathed, plumed, hatted or wigged, but masked,—
Always masked,—only, how? No face-shape, beast or bird,
Nay, fish and reptile even, but some one had preferred,
From out its frontispiece, feathered or scaled or curled,
To make the vizard whence himself should view the world,
And where the world believed himself was manifest.
Yet, when you came to look, mixed up among the rest
More funnily by far were masks to imitate
Humanity's mishap: the wrinkled brow, bald pate,
And rheumy eyes of Age, peaked chin and parchment chap,
Were signs of day-work done, and wage-time near,—mishap
Merely; but Age reduced to simple greed and guile,
Worn apathetic else as some smooth slab, erewhile

A clear-cut man-at-arms i' the pavement, till foot's tread
Effaced the sculpture, left the stone you saw instead, —
Was not that terrible beyond the mere uncouth?
Well, and perhaps the next revolting you was Youth,
Stark ignorance and crude conceit, half smirk, half stare,
On that frank fool-face, gay beneath its head of hair
Which covers nothing.

XCVI.

These, you are to understand,
Were the mere hard and sharp distinctions. On each hand,
I soon became aware, flocked the infinitude
Of passions, loves and hates, man pampers till his mood
Becomes himself, the whole sole face we name him by,
Nor want denotement else, if age or youth supply
The rest of him: old, young, — classed creature: in the main
A love, a hate, a hope, a fear, each soul a-strain

Some one way through the flesh,— the face the evidence
O' the soul at work inside; and, all the more intense,
So much the more grotesque.

XCVII.

"Why should each soul be tasked
Some one way, by one love or else one hate?" I asked;
When it occurred to me, from all these sights beneath
There rose not any sound: a crowd, yet dumb as death!

XCVIII.

But I knew why. (Propose a riddle, and 'tis solved
Forthwith — in dream!) They spoke; but — since on me devolved
To see, and understand by sight — the vulgar speech
Might be dispensed with. "He who cannot see must reach
As best he may the truth of men by help of words
They please to speak; must fare at will of who affords

The banquet:" so I thought. "Who sees not, hears, and so
Gets to believe: myself it is, that, seeing, know,
And, knowing, can dispense with voice and vanity
Of speech. What hinders then, that, drawing closer, I
Put privilege to use, see and know better still
These *simulachra*, taste the profit of my skill,
Down in the midst?"

XCIX.

And plumb I pitched into the square,—
A groundling like the rest. What think you happened there?
Precise the contrary of what one would expect!
For—whereas all the more monstrosities deflect
From nature and the type the more yourself approach
Their precinct—here I found brutality encroach
Less on the human, lie the lightlier as I looked
The nearer on these faces that seemed but now so crooked

And clawed away from God's prime purpose. They
diverged
A little from the type, but somehow rather urged
To pity than disgust: the prominent before
Now dwindled into mere distinctness, — nothing more.
Still, at first sight, stood forth undoubtedly the fact
Some deviation was: in no one case there lacked
The certain sign and mark, say hint, say trick of lip
Or twist of nose, that proved a fault in workmanship,
Change in the prime design, some hesitancy here
And there, which checked man's make, and let the beast
appear;
But that was all.

C.

All; yet enough to bid each tongue
Lie in abeyance still. They talked, themselves among,
Of themselves, to themselves: I saw the mouths at play,
The gesture that enforced, the eye that strove to say
The same thing as the voice, and seldom gained its
point:
That this was so, I saw; but all seemed out of joint

I' the vocal medium 'twixt the world and me. I gained
Knowledge by notice, not by giving ear; attained
To truth by what men seemed, not said: to me one glance
Was worth whole histories of noisy utterance;
At least, to me in dream.

CI.

And presently I found,
That, just as ugliness had withered, so unwound
Itself, and perished off, repugnance to what wrong
Might linger yet i' the make of man. My will was strong
I' the matter: I could pick and choose, project my weight,
(Remember how we saw the boatman trim his freight!)
Determine to observe, or manage to escape,
Or make divergency assume another shape
By shift of point of sight in me the observer: thus
Corrected, added to, subtracted from, discuss
Each variant quality, and brute-beast touch was turned
Into mankind's safeguard! Force, guile, were arms which earned

My praise, not blame at all! for we must learn to live,
Case-hardened at all points, not bare and sensitive,
But plated for defence, nay, furnished for attack,
With spikes at the due place, that neither front nor back
May suffer in that squeeze with nature we find — life.
Are we not here to learn the good of peace through strife,
Of love through hate, and reach knowledge by ignorance?
Why, those are helps thereto which late we eyed askance,
And nicknamed unaware! Just so, a sword we call
Superfluous, and cry out against, at festival:
Wear it in time of war, its clink and clatter grate
O' the ear to purpose then!

CII.

I found one must abate
One's scorn of the soul's case, distinct from the soul's self, —
Which is the centre-drop; whereas the pride in pelf,

The lust to seem the thing it cannot be, the greed
For praise, and all the rest seen outside, — these, indeed,
Are the hard polished cold crystal environment
Of those strange orbs unearthed i' the Druid temple, meant
For divination (so the learned lean to think),
Wherein you may admire one dew-drop roll and wink,
All unaffected by — quite alien to — what sealed
And saved it long ago: though how it got congealed
I shall not give a guess; nor how, by power occult,
The solid surface-shield was outcome and result
Of simple dew at work to save itself amid
The unwatery force around: protected thus, dew slid
Safe through all opposites impatient to absorb
Its spot of life, and lasts forever in the orb
We now from hand to hand pass with impunity.

CIII.

And the delight wherewith I watch this crowd must be
Akin to that which crowns the chemist when he winds
Thread up and up till clew be fairly clutched; unbinds

The composite; ties fast the simple to its mate;
And, tracing each effect back to its cause, elate,
Constructs in fancy, from the fewest primitives,
The complex and complete, all diverse life, that lives
Not only in beast, bird, fish, reptile, insect, but
The very plants and earths and ores. Just so I glut
My hunger both to be and know the thing I am
By contrast with the thing I am not; so, through sham
And outside, I arrive at inmost real, probe
And prove how the nude form obtained the checkered
robe.

CIV.

—Experience I am glad to master soon or late,
Here, there, and everywhere i' the world, without debate;
Only in Venice why? What reason for Mark's Square
Rather than Timbuctoo?

CV.

And I became aware,
Scarcely the word escaped my lips, that swift ensued
In silence and by stealth, and yet with certitude,

A formidable change of the amphitheatre
Which held the Carnival; although the human stir
Continued just the same amid that shift of scene.

CVI.

For as on edifice of cloud i' the gray and green
Of evening, — built about some glory of the west
To barricade the sun's departure, — manifest,
He plays, pre-eminently gold, gilds vapor, crag, and crest
Which bend in rapt suspense above the act and deed
They cluster round and keep their very own, nor heed
The world at watch; while we, breathlessly at the base
O' the castellated bulk, note momently the mace
Of night fall here, fall there, bring change with every blow,
Alike to sharpened shaft and broadened portico
I' the structure; heights and depths, beneath the leaden stress,
Crumble and melt and mix together, coalesce,
Re-form, but sadder still, subdued yet more and more
By every fresh defeat, till wearied eyes need pore

No longer on the dull impoverished decadence
Of all that pomp of pile in towering evidence
So lately: —

CVII.

Even thus, nor otherwise, meseemed
That if I fixed my gaze a while on what I dreamed
Was Venice' Square, Mark's Church, the scheme was straight unschemed,
A subtle something had its way within the heart
Of each and every house I watched, with counterpart
Of tremor through the front and outward face, until
Mutation was at end: impassive and stock-still
Stood now the ancient house, grown, — new is scarce the phrase,
Since older, in a sense, — altered to — what i' the ways
Ourselves are won't to see, coerced by city, town,
Or village, anywhere i' the world, pace up or down
Europe! In all the maze, no single tenement
I saw, but I could claim acquaintance with!

CVIII.

There went
Conviction to my soul, that what I took of late
For Venice was the world; its Carnival the state
Of mankind, masquerade in life-long permanence
For all time, and no one particular feast-day. Whence
'Twas easy to infer what meant my late disgust
At the brute-pageant, each grotesque of greed and lust
And idle hate, and love as impotent for good,
When from my pride of place I passed the interlude
In critical review; and what the wonder that ensued,
When, from such pinnacled pre-eminence, I found
Somehow the proper goal for wisdom was the ground,
And not the sky, — so, slid sagaciously betimes
Down heaven's baluster-rope, to reach the mob of mimes
And mummers; whereby came discovery there was just
Enough and not too much of hate, love, greed, and lust,
Could one discerningly but hold the balance, shift
The weight from scale to scale, do justice to the drift
Of nature, and explain the glories by the shames
Mixed up in man, one stuff miscalled by different names,

According to what stage i' the process turned his rough,
Even as I gazed, to smooth, — only get close enough! —
What was all this except the lesson of a life?

CIX.

And consequent upon the learning how from strife
Grew peace, — from evil, good, — came knowledge, that, to get
Acquaintance with the way o' the world, we must nor fret
Nor fume on altitudes of self-sufficiency,
But bid a frank farewell to what — we think — should be,
And, with as good a grace, welcome what is — we find.

CX.

Is — for the hour, observe! Since something to my mind
Suggested soon the fancy, nay, certitude, that change,
Never suspending touch, continued to derange
What architecture, we, walled up within the cirque
O' the world, consider fixed as fate, not fairy-work.

For those were temples, sure, which tremblingly grew blank
From bright, then broke afresh in triumph: ah! but sank
As soon; for liquid change through artery and vein
O' the very marble wound its way! And first a stain
Would startle and offend amid the glory; next
Spot swift succeeded spot, but found me less perplexed
By potents; then, as 'twere, a sleepiness soft stole
Over the stately fane, and shadow sucked the whole
Façade into itself, made uniformly earth
What was a piece of heaven; till, lo! a second birth,
And the veil broke away because of something new
Inside, that pushed to gain an outlet, paused in view
At last, and proved a growth of stone or brick or wood,
Which, alien to the aim o' the Builder, somehow stood
The test, could satisfy, if not the early race
For whom he built, at least our present populace,
Who must not bear the blame for what, blamed, proves mishap
Of the Artist: his work gone, another fills the gap,

Serves the prime purpose so. Undoubtedly there spreads
Building around, above, which makes men lift their heads
To look at, or look through, or look, for aught I care,
Over, — if only up it is, not down, they stare,
"Commercing with the skies," and not the pavement in the square.

CXI.

But are they only temples that subdivide, collapse,
And tower again, transformed? Academies, perhaps!
Domes where dwells Learning, seats of Science, bower and hall
Which house Philosophy, — do these, too, rise and fall,
Based though foundations be on steadfast mother-earth,
With no chimeric claim to supermundane birth;
No boast, that, dropped from cloud, they did not grow from ground?
Why, these fare worst of all! these vanish, and are found
Nowhere, by who tasks eye some twice within his term
Of threescore years and ten for tidings what each germ

Has burgeoned out into, whereof the promise stunned
His ear with such acclaim, — praise-payment to refund
The praises, never doubt, some twice before they die
Whose days are long i' the land.

CXII.

Alack, Philosophy!
Despite the chop and change, diminished or increased,
Patched up and plastered o'er, Religion stands at least
I' the temple-type. But thou? Here gape I, all agog
These thirty years, to learn how tadpole turns to frog;
And thrice at least have gazed with mild astonishment,
As, skyward up and up, some fire-new fabric sent
Its challenge to mankind, that, clustered underneath, —
They hear the word and straight believe, ay, in the teeth
O' the Past, clap hands, and hail triumphant Truth's outbreak, —
Tadpole-frog-theory propounded past mistake!
In vain! A something ails the edifice: it bends,
It bows, it buries. . . . Haste! cry "Heads below" to friends;

But have no fear they find, when smother shall subside,
Some substitution perk with unabated pride
I' the predecessor's place!

CXIII.

No: the one voice which failed
Never, the preachment's coigne of vantage nothing ailed,—
That had the luck to lodge i' the house not made with hands!
And all it preached was this: "Truth builds upon the sands,
Though stationed on a rock; and so her work decays,
And so she builds afresh, with like result. Nought stays
But just the fact that Truth not only is, but fain
Would have men know she needs must be, by each so plain
Attempt to visibly inhabit where they dwell."
Her works are work, while she is she: that work does well

Which lasts mankind their lifetime through, and lets
believe
One generation more, that, though sand run through
sieve,
Yet earth now reached is rock, and what we moderns
find
Erected here is Truth, who, 'stablished to her mind
I' the fulness of the days, will never change in show
More than in substance erst: men thought they knew;
we know!

CXIV.

Do you, my generation? Well, let the blocks prove
mist
I' the main enclosure; church and college, if they list,
Be something for a time, and every thing anon,
And any thing a while, as fit is off or on,
Till they grow nothing, soon to re-appear no less
As something, — shape reshaped, till out of shapeless-
ness
Come shape again as sure! no doubt, or round or square
Or polygon its front, some building will be there,

Do duty in that nook o' the wall o' the world where once
The Architect saw fit precisely to ensconce
College or church, and bid such bulwark guard the line
O' the barrier round about,—humanity's confine.

CXV.

Leave watching change at work i' the greater scale, on these
The main supports, and turn to their interstices
Filled up by fabrics too, less costly and less rare,
Yet of importance, yet essential to the Fair
They help to circumscribe, instruct, and regulate!
See where each booth-front boasts, in letters small or great,
Its specialty, proclaims its privilege to stop
A breach beside the best!

CXVI.

Here History keeps shop;
Tells how past deeds were done, so and not otherwise:—
"Man, hold truth evermore! forget the early lies!"

There sits Morality, demure behind her stall,
Dealing out life and death: "This is the thing to call
Right; and this other, wrong: thus think, thus do, thus say,
Thus joy, thus suffer! — not to-day as yesterday:
Yesterday's doctrine dead, this only shall endure!
Obey its voice, and live!" — enjoins the dame demure.
While Art gives flag to breeze, bids drum beat, trumpet blow,
Inviting eye and ear to yonder raree-show.
Up goes the canvas, hauled to height of pole. I think
We know the way — long lost, late learned — to paint! A wink
Of eye, and, lo, the pose! the statue on its plinth!
How could we moderns miss the heart o' the labyrinth
Perversely all these years, permit the Greek seclude
His secret till to-day? And here's another feud
Now happily composed: inspect this quartet-score!
Got long past melody, no word has Music more

To say to mortal man! But is the bard to be
Behindhand? Here's his book; and now perhaps you see,
At length, what poetry can do!

CXVII.

Why, that's stability
Itself, that change on change we sorrowfully saw
Creep o'er the prouder piles! We acquiesced in law
When the fine gold grew dim i' the temple; when the brass
Which pillared that so brave abode where Knowledge was
Bowed and resigned the trust: but bear all this caprice,
Harlequinade where swift to birth succeeds decease
Of hue at every turn o' the tinsel-flag which flames
While Art holds booth in Fair? Such glories chased by shames
Like these distract beyond the solemn and august
Procedure to decay, evanishment in dust,
Of those marmoreal domes, — above vicissitude,
We used to hope!

CXVIII.

"So all is change, in fine," pursued
The preachment to a pause. When — "All is permanence!"
Returned a voice. Within? without? No matter whence
The explanation came; for, understand, I ought
To simply say — I saw, each thing I say I thought.
Since ever as, unrolled, the strange scene-picture grew
Before me, sight flashed first, though mental comment too
Would follow in a trice, come hobblingly to halt.

CXIX.

So what did I see next, but, — much as when the vault
I' the west, — wherein we watch the vapory, manifold
Transfiguration, — tired would turn to rest, — behold,
Peak reconciled to base, dark ending feud with bright,
The multiform subsides, is found the definite.
Contrasting lives and strifes, where battle they i' the blank
Severity of death and peace, for which we thank

One cloud that comes to quell the concourse, fall at last
Into a shape befits the close of things, and cast
Palpably o'er vexed earth heaven's mantle of repose?

CXX.

Just so, in Venice' Square, that things were at the close
Was signalled to my sense; for I perceived arrest
O' the change all round about. As if some impulse pressed
Each gently into each, what was distinctness late
Grew vague, and, line from line no longer separate,
No matter what the style, edifice — shall I say,
Died into edifice? I find no simpler way
Of saying how, without or dash or shock or trace
Of violence, I found unity in the place
Of temple, tower, and hall and house and hut, — one blank
Severity of death and peace; to which they sank
Resigned enough, till — ah! conjecture, I beseech,
What special blank did they agree to, all and each?

What common shape was that wherein they mutely merged
Likes and dislikes of form, so plain before?

CXXI.

I urged
Your step this way, prolonged our path of enterprise
To where we stand at last, in order that your eyes
Might see the very thing, and save my tongue describe
The Druid monument which fronts you. Could I bribe
Nature to come in aid, illustrate what I mean,
What wants there she would lend to solemnize the scene?

CXXII.

How does it strike you, this construction gaunt and gray?
Sole object, these piled stones, that gleam unground away
By twilight's hungry jaw, which champs fine all beside
I' the solitary waste we grope through. Oh, no guide,

However, need we now to reach the monstrous door
Of granite! Take my word, the deeper you explore
That caverned passage, filled with fancies to the brim,
The less will you approve the adventure! such a grim
Bar-sinister soon blocks abrupt your path, and ends
All with a cold dread shape, — shape whereon Learning spends
Labor, and leaves the text obscurer for the gloss;
While Ignorance reads right, — recoiling from that Cross!
Whence came the mass and mass, strange quality of stone
Unquarried anywhere i' the region round? Unknown!
Just as unknown how such enormity could be
Conveyed by land, or else transported over sea,
And laid in order, so, precisely each on each
As you and I would build a grotto where the beach
Sheds shell, — to last an hour: this building lasts from age
To age the same. But why?

CXXIII.

Ask Learning! I engage
You get a prosy wherefore shall help you to advance
In knowledge just as much as helps you Ignorance
Surmising, in the mouth of peasant lad or lass,—
"I heard my father say he understood it was
A building people built as soon as earth was made
Almost, because they might forget (they were afraid)
Earth did not make itself, but came of Somebody.
They labored that their work might last, and show thereby
He stays, while we and earth and all things come and go.
Come whence? Go whither? That, when come and gone, we know,
Perhaps, but not while earth and all things need our best
Attention: we must wait and die to know the rest.
Ask, if that's true, what use in setting up the pile?
To make one fear and hope; remind us, all the while
We come and go, outside there's Somebody that stays,—
A circumstance which ought to make us mind our ways;

Because, — whatever end we answer by this life, —
Next time, best chance must be for who with toil and strife
Manages now to live most like what he was meant
Become: since who succeeds so far, 'tis evident,
Stands foremost on the file; who fails has less to hope
From new promotion. That's the rule, — with even a rope
Of mushrooms like this rope I dangle! those that grew
Greatest and roundest, all in life they had to do,
Gain a reward, a grace they never dreamed, I think;
Since, outside white as milk, and inside black as ink,
They go to the Great House to make a dainty dish
For Don and Donna; while this basket-load, I wish
Well off my arm, it breaks, — no starveling of the heap
But had his share of dew, his proper length of sleep
I' the sunshine: yet, of all, the outcome is, — this queer
Cribbed quantity of dwarfs which burthen basket here
Till I reach home; 'tis there, that, having run their rigs,
They end their earthly race, are flung as food for pigs.

Any more use I see? Well, you must know, there lies
Something, the curé says, that points to mysteries
Above our grasp: a huge stone pillar, once upright,
Now laid at length, half lost, — discreetly shunning sight
I' the bush and brier, because of stories in the air, —
Hints what it signified, and why was stationed there,
Once on a time. In vain the curé tasked his lungs;
Showed, in a preachment, how, at bottom of the rungs
O' the ladder Jacob saw, where heavenly angels stept
Up and down, lay a stone which served him, while he slept,
For pillow; when he woke, he set the same upright
As pillar, and atop poured oil: things requisite
To instruct posterity, there mounts from floor to roof
A staircase, earth to heaven; and also put in proof,
When we have scaled the sky, we well may let alone
What raised us from the ground, and — paying to the stone
Proper respect, of course — take staff and go our way,
Leaving the Pagan night for Christian break of day.

'For,' preached he, 'what they dreamed, these Pagans, wide-awake,
We Christians may behold. How strange, then, were mistake,
Did anybody style the stone — because of drop
Remaining there from oil which Jacob poured atop —
Itself the Gate of Heaven; itself the end, and not
The means thereto!' Thus preached the curé, and no jot
The more persuaded people, but that, what once a thing
Meant, and had right to mean, it still must mean. So cling
Folk somehow to the prime authoritative speech,
And so distrust report, it seems as they could reach
Far better the arch-word, whereon their fate depends,
Through rude charactery, than all the grace it lends,
That lettering of your scribes! who flourish pen apace,
And ornament the text, they say; we say, efface.
Hence, when the earth began its life afresh in May,
And fruit-trees bloomed, and waves would wanton, and the bay

Ruffle its wealth of weed, and stranger-birds arrive,
And beasts take each a mate, — folk, too, found sensitive,
Surmised the old gray stone upright there, through such tracts
Of solitariness and silence, kept the facts
Intrusted it, could deal out doctrine, did it please:
No fresh and frothy draught, but liquor on the lees,
Strong, savage, and sincere, — first bleedings from a vine,
Whereof the product now do curés so refine
To insipidity, that, when heart sinks, we strive
And strike from out the old stone the old restorative.
'Which is?' — why, go and ask our grandams how they used
To dance around it, till the curé disabused
Their ignorance, and bade the parish in a band
Lay flat the obtrusive thing that cumbered so the land!
And there, accordingly, in bush and brier, it — 'bides
Its time to rise again' (so somebody derides,
That's pert from Paris); 'since yon spire, you keep erect
Yonder, and pray beneath, is nothing, I suspect,

But just the symbol's self, expressed in slate for rock,—
Art's smooth for Nature's rough, new chip from the old block!'
There, sir, my say is said! Thanks, and Saint Gille increase
The wealth bestowed so well!"—wherewith he pockets piece,
Doffs cap, and takes the road. I leave in Learning's clutch
More money for his book, but scarcely gain as much.

CXXIV.

To this it was, this same primeval monument,
That, in my dream, I saw building with building blent
Fall: each on each they fast and founderingly went
Confusion-ward; but thence again subsided fast,
Became the mound you see. Magnificently massed
Indeed, those mammoth-stones, piled by the Protoplast
Temple-wise in my dream! beyond compare with fanes,
Which, solid-looking late, had left no least remains
I' the bald and blank, now sole usurper of the plains

Of heaven, diversified and beautiful before.
And yet simplicity appeared to speak no more
Nor less to me than spoke the compound. At the core,
One and no other word, as in the crust of late,
Whispered, which, audible through the transition-state,
Was no loud utterance in even the ultimate
Disposure. For as some imperial chord subsists,
Steadily underlies the accidental mists
Of music springing thence, that run their mazy race
Around, and sink, absorbed, back to the triad base;
So, out of that one word, each variant rose and fell,
And left the same "All's change, but permanence as well."
Grave note, whence — list aloft! — harmonics sound, that mean, —
"Truth inside; and, outside, truth also; and, between
Each, falsehood that is change, as truth is permanence.
The individual soul works through the shows of sense
(Which, ever proving false, still promise to be true)
Up to an outer soul as individual too;

And, through the fleeting, lives to die into the fixed,
And reach at length 'God, man, or both together mixed,'
Transparent through the flesh, by parts which prove a whole,
By hints which make the soul discernible by soul, —
Let only soul look up, not down, not hate, but love,
As truth successively takes shape, one grade above
Its last presentment, tempts as it were truth indeed
Revealed this time; so tempts, till we attain to read
The signs aright, and learn, by failure, truth is forced
To manifest itself through falsehood; whence divorced
By the excepted eye, at the rare season, for
The happy moment, truth instructs us to abhor
The false, and prize the true, obtainable thereby.
Then do we understand the value of a lie:
Its purpose served, its truth once safe deposited,
Each lie, superfluous now, leaves, in the singer's stead,
The indubitable song; the historic personage
Put by, leaves prominent the impulse of his age;

Truth sets aside speech, act, time, place, indeed, but
brings
Nakedly forward now the principle of things
Highest and least."

CXXV.

Wherewith change ends. What
other change to dread,
When, disengaged at last from every veil, instead
Of type remains the truth? Once — falsehood; but
anon
Theosuton e broteion eper kekramenon, —
Something as true as soul is true, though veils be-
tween
Are false, and fleet away. As I mean, did he mean,
The poet whose bird-phrase sits, singing in my ear
A mystery not unlike? What through the dark and
drear
Brought comfort to the Titan? Emerging from the
lymph,
"God, man, or mixture," proved only to be a nymph:

"From whom the clink on clink of metal" (money, judged
Abundant in my purse) "struck" (bumped at, till it budged)
"The modesty, her soul's habitual resident,"
Where late the sisterhood were lively in their tent,)
"As out of wingèd car" (that caravan on wheels)
"Impulsively she rushed, no slippers to her heels,"
And "Fear not, friends we flock!" soft smiled the sea-Fifine,—
Primitive of the veils (if he meant what I mean)
The poet's Titan learned to lift, ere "Three-formed Fate,
Moirai Trimorphoi," stood unmasked the Ultimate.

CXXVI.

Enough o' the dream! You see how poetry turns prose.
Announcing wonder-work, I dwindle at the close
Down to mere commonplace which everybody knows.
But dreaming disappoints. The fresh and strange at first
Soon wear to trite and tame, nor warrant the outburst

Of heart with which we hail those heights, at very brink
Of heaven, whereto one least of lifts would lead, we think;
But wherefrom quick decline conducts our step, we find,
To homely earth, and fact familiar left behind.
Did not this monument, for instance, long ago
Say all it had to say, show all it had to show,
Nor promise to do duty more in dream?

CXXVII.

Awaking so,
What if we, homeward-bound, all peace and some fatigue,
Trudge, soberly complete our tramp of near a league,
Last little mile which makes the circuit just, Elvire?
We end where we began: that consequence is clear.
All peace and some fatigue, wherever we were nursed
To life, we bosom us on death, find last is first,
And thenceforth final too.

CXXVIII.

"Why final? Why the more
Worth credence now than when such truth proved false
before?"
Because a novel point impresses now: each lie
Redounded to the praise of man, was victory
Man's nature had both right to get, and might to gain,
And by no means implied submission to the reign
Of other quite as real a nature, that saw fit
To have its way with man, not man its way with it.
This time, acknowledgment and acquiescence quell
Their contrary in man; promotion proves as well
Defeat; and Truth, unlike the False with Truth's outside,
Neither plumes up his will, nor puffs him out with pride.
I fancy there must lurk some cogency i' the claim,
Man, such abatement made, submits to, all the same.
Soul finds no triumph, here, to register like Sense,
With whom 'tis ask and have,—the want, the evidence
That the thing wanted, soon or late will be supplied.
This indeed plumes up will, this, sure, puffs out with
pride,

When, reading records right, man's instincts still attest
Promotion comes to Sense because Sense likes it best:
For bodies sprouted legs, through a desire to run;
While hands, when fain to filch, got fingers one by one;
And nature, that's ourself, accommodative brings
To bear, that, tired of legs which walk, we now bud wings,
Since of a mind to fly. Such savor in the nose
Of Sense would stimulate Soul sweetly, I suppose, —
Soul with its proper itch of instinct, prompting clear
To recognize Soul's self Soul's only master here
Alike from first to last. But if time's pressure, light's,
Or rather dark's, approach, wrest thoroughly the rights
Of rule away, and bid the soul submissive bear
Another soul than it play master everywhere
In great and small, — this time, I fancy, none disputes
There's something in the fact that such conclusion suits
Nowise the pride of man, nor yet chimes in with attributes
Conspicuous in the lord of nature. He receives,
And not demands, — not first likes faith, and then believes.

CXXIX.

And as with the last essence, so with its first faint
type.
Inconstancy means raw; 'tis faith alone means ripe
I' the soul which runs its round: no matter how it
range
From Helen to Fifine, Elvire bids back the change
To permanence. Here, too, love ends where love
began.
Such ending looks like law, because the natural man
Inclines the other way, feels lordlier free than bound.
Poor pabulum for pride when the first love is found
Last also! and, so far from realizing gain,
Each step aside just proves divergency in vain.
The wanderer brings home no profit from his quest
Beyond the sad surmise that keeping house were
best
Could life begin anew. His problem posed aright
Was, "From the given point evolve the infinite!"
Not, "Spend thyself in space, endeavoring to joint
Together, and so make infinite, point and point:

Fix into one Elvire a Fair-ful of Fifines!"
Fifine, the foam-flake, she: Elvire, the sea's self, means
Capacity at need to shower how many such!
And yet we left her calm profundity, to clutch
Foam-flutter, bell on bell, that, bursting at a touch,
Blistered us for our pains. But, wise, we want no more
O' the fickle element. Enough of foam and roar!
Land-locked, we live and die henceforth; for here's the villa-door.

CXXX.

How pallidly you pause o' the threshold! Hardly night,
Which drapes you, ought to make real flesh and blood so white!
Touch me, and so appear alive to all intents!
Will the saint vanish from the sinner that repents?
Suppose you are a ghost! — a memory, a hope,
A fear, a conscience! Quick! — give back the hand I grope
I' the dusk for!

CXXXI.

That is well. Our double horoscope
I cast, while you concur. Discard that simile
O' the fickle element! Elvire is land, not sea, —
The solid land, the safe. All these word-bubbles came
O' the sea, and bite like salt. The unlucky bath's to blame.
This hand of yours on heart of mine, no more the bay
I beat, nor bask beneath the blue! In Pornic, say,
The mayor shall catalogue me duly domiciled,
Contributable, good-companion of the guild
And mystery of marriage. I stickle for the town,
And not this tower apart; because, though, half way down,
Its mullions wink o'er-webbed with bloomy greenness yet,
Who mounts to staircase top may tempt the parapet,
And sudden there's the sea! No memories to arouse,
No fancies to delude! Our honest civic house
Of the earth be earthy too! — or graced perchance with shell
Made prize of long ago, picked haply where the swell

Menaced a little once; or seaweed-branch that yet
Dampens and softens, notes a freak of wind, a fret
Of wave: though why on earth should sea-change mend or mar
The calm contemplative householders that we are?
So shall the seasons fleet, while our two selves abide:
E'en past astonishment how sunrise and springtide
Could tempt one forth to swim; the more if time appoints
That swimming grow a task for one's rheumatic joints.
Such honest civic house, behold, I constitute
Our villa! Be but flesh and blood, and smile to boot!
Enter for good and all! then fate bolt fast the door,
Shut you and me inside, never to wander more!

CXXXII.

Only, you do not use to apprehend attack!
No doubt, the way I march, one idle arm, thrown slack
Behind me, leaves the open hand defenceless at the back,

Should an impertinent on tiptoe steal, and stuff—
Whatever can it be? A letter sure enough,
Pushed betwixt palm and glove! That largess of a
franc?
Perhaps inconsciously,—to better help the blank
O' the nest, her tambourine, and, laying egg, persuade
A family to follow, the nest-egg that I laid
May have contained—but just to foil suspicious folk—
Between two silver whites a yellow double yolk!
Oh, threaten no farewell! five minutes shall suffice
To clear the matter up. I go, and in a trice
Return; five minutes past, expect me! If in vain,—
Why, slip from flesh and blood, and play the ghost
again!

EPILOGUE.

THE HOUSEHOLDER.

I.

SAVAGE I was sitting in my house, ate, lone;
  Dreary, weary with the long day's work;
Head of me, heart of me, stupid as a stone;
  Tongue-tied now, now blaspheming like a Turk;
When, in a moment, just a knock, call, cry,
  Half a pang, and all a rapture, there again were we!
"What, and is it really you again?" quoth I.
  "I again; what else did you expect?" quoth She.

II.

"Never mind: hie away from this old house,—
  Every crumbling brick imbrowned with sin and shame!
Quick! in its corners ere certain shapes arouse!
  Let them—every devil of the night—lay claim,
Make and mend, or rap and rend, for me! Good-by!
  God be their guard from disturbance at their glee,
Till, crash, comes down the carcass in a heap!" quoth I.
  "Nay; but there's a decency required!" quoth She.

III.

"Ah, but if you knew how time has dragged, days, nights!
  All the neighbor-talk with man and maid,—such men!
All the fuss and trouble of street-sounds, window-sights;
  All the worry of flapping door and echoing roof; and, then,
All the fancies. . . . Who were they had leave, dared try
  Darker arts that almost struck despair in me?
If you knew but how I dwelt down here!" quoth I.
  "And was I so better off up there?" quoth She.

IV.

"Help and get it over! *Re-united to his wife,*
  (How draw up the paper lets the parish-people know?)
Lies M. or N., departed from this life,
  Day the this or that, month and year the so and so.

What i' the way of final flourish? Prose, verse? Try!
Affliction sore long time he bore, or what is it to be?
Till God did please to grant him ease. Do end!" quoth I.
"I end with—Love is all, and Death is nought!" quoth She.

PRINCE HOHENSTIEL-SCHWANGAU,

SAVIOUR OF SOCIETY.

Ὕδραν φονεύσας, μυρίων τ' ἄλλων πόνων
διῆλθον ἀγέλας . . .
τὸ λοίσθιον δὲ τόνδ' ἔτλην τάλας πόνον,
. . . δῶμα θριγκῶσαι κακοῖς.

I slew the Hydra, and from labor passed
To labor, — tribes of labors ! Till at last,
Attempting one more labor, in a trice,
Alack ! with ills I *crowned the edifice.*

PRINCE HOHENSTIEL-SCHWANGAU,

SAVIOUR OF SOCIETY.

YOU have seen better days, dear? So have I, —
And worse too; for they brought no such bud-mouth
As yours to lisp, "You wish you knew me!" Well,
Wise men, 'tis said, have sometimes wished the same,
And wished and had their trouble for their pains.
Suppose my Œdipus should lurk at last
Under a pork-pie hat and crinoline,
And, latish, pounce on Sphinx in Leicester Square?
Or, likelier, what if Sphinx in wise old age,
Grown sick of snapping foolish people's heads,
And jealous for her riddle's proper rede, —

Jealous that the good trick which served the turn
Have justice rendered it, nor class one day
With friend Home's stilts and tongs and medium-ware, —
What if the once redoubted Sphinx, I say,
(Because night draws on, and the sands increase,
And desert-whispers grow a prophecy,)
Tell all to Corinth of her own accord,
Bright Corinth, not dull Thebes, for Laïs' sake,
Who finds me hardly gray, and likes my nose,
And thinks a man of sixty at the prime?
Good! It shall be! Revealment of myself!
But listen; for we must co-operate.
I don't drink tea: permit me the cigar.

First, how to make the matter plain, of course, —
What was the law by which I lived. Let's see:
Ay, we must take one instant of my life
Spent sitting by your side in this neat room:
Watch well the way I use it, and don't laugh.
Here's paper on the table, pen and ink:
Give me the soiled bit, not the pretty rose.

See! having sat an hour, I'm rested now,
Therefore want work; and spy no better work
For eye and hand, and mind that guides them both,
During this instant, than to draw my pen
From blot One — thus — up, up to blot Two — thus —
Which I at last reach, thus; and here's my line
Five inches long, and tolerably straight.
Better to draw than leave undrawn, I think;
Fitter to do than let alone, I hold;
Though better, fitter, by but one degree.
Therefore it was, that, rather than sit still
Simply, my right hand drew it while my left
Pulled smooth and pinched the mustache to a point.

Now I permit your plump lips to unpurse: —
" So far, one possibly may understand
Without recourse to witchcraft." True, my dear.
Thus folks begin with Euclid; finish, how?
Trying to square the circle! — at any rate,
Solving abstruser problems than this first,—
" How find the nearest way 'twixt point and point."

Deal but with moral mathematics so;
Master one merest moment's work of mine,
Even this practising with pen and ink;
Demonstrate why I rather plied the quill
Than left the space a blank, — you gain a fact;
And God knows what a fact's worth! So proceed
By inference from just this moral fact;
I don't say to that plaguy quadrature,
"What the whole man meant, whom you wish you knew,"
But what meant certain things he did of old
Which puzzled Europe; why, you'll find them plain,
This way, not otherwise: I guarantee,
Understand one, you comprehend the rest.
Rays from all round converge to any point:
Study the point, then, ere you track the rays.
The size o' the circle's nothing: subdivide
Earth, and earth's smallest grain of mustard-seed,
You count as many parts, small matching large,
If you can use the mind's eye; otherwise,
Material optics, being gross at best,
Prefer the large, and leave our mind the small.

And pray how many folks have minds can see?
Certainly you, and somebody in Thrace
Whose name escapes me at the moment. You —
Lend me your mind, then. Analyze with me
This instance of the line 'twixt blot and blot
I rather chose to draw than leave a blank,
Things else being equal. You are taught thereby
That 'tis my nature, when I am at ease,
Rather than idle out my life too long,
To want to do a thing, to put a thought,
Whether a great thought or a little one,
Into an act, as nearly as may be.
Make what is absolutely new, I can't;
Mar what is made already well enough,
I won't: but turn to best account the thing
That's half made, that I can. Two blots you saw
I knew how to extend into a line
Symmetric on the sheet they blurred before:
Such little act sufficed, this time, such thought.

Now we'll extend rays, widen out the verge,

Describe a larger circle, leave this first
Clod of an instance we began with, rise
To the complete world many clods effect.
Only continue patient while I throw,
Delver-like, spadeful after spadeful up,
Just as truths come, the subsoil of me, mould
Whence spring my moods : your object, — just to find,
Alike from hand-lift and from barrow-load,
What salts and silts may constitute the earth,
If it be proper stuff to blow man glass,
Or bake him pottery, bear him oaks or wheat;
What's born of me, in brief; which found, all's known.
If it were genius did the digging job,
Logic would speedily sift its product smooth,
And leave the crude truths bare for poetry;
But I'm no poet, and am stiff i' the back.
What one spread fails to bring, another may.
In goes the shovel, and out comes scoop, — as here!

I live to please myself. I recognize
Power passing mine, immeasurable, God, —

Above me whom he made, as heaven beyond
Earth, — to use figures which assist our sense.
I know that he is there as I am here,
By the same proof, which seems no proof at all,
It so exceeds familiar forms of proof.
Why "there," not "here"? Because, when I say "there,"
I treat the feeling with distincter shape
That space exists between us; I, not he,
Live, think, do human work here: no machine
His will moves, but a being by myself,
His, and not he who made me for a work,
Watches my working, judges its effect,
But does not interpose. He did so once,
And probably will again some time, not now,
Life being the minute of mankind, not God's,
In a certain sense, like time before and time
After man's earthly life, so far as man
Needs apprehend the matter. Am I clear?
Suppose I bid a courier take to-night, —
(Once for all, let me talk as if I smoked
Yet in the Residenz, a personage:

I must still represent the thing I was,
Galvanically make dead muscle play,
Or how shall I illustrate muscle's use?) —
I could then, last July, bid courier take
Message for me, post-haste, a thousand miles.
I bid him, since I have the right to bid;
And, my part done so far, his part begins.
He starts with due equipment, will and power,
Means he may use, misuse, not use at all,
At his discretion, at his peril too.
I leave him to himself: but, journey done,
I count the minutes, call for the result
In quickness and the courier quality,
Weigh its worth, and then punish or reward
According to proved service; not before.
Meantime he sleeps through noontide, rides till dawn,
Sticks to the straight road, tries the crooked path,
Measures and manages resource, trusts, doubts
Advisers by the wayside, does his best
At his discretion, lags, or launches forth
(He knows and I know) at his peril too.

You see? Exactly thus men stand to God, —
I with my courier, God with me. Just so
I have his bidding to perform; but mind
And body, all of me, though made and meant
For that sole service, must consult, concert,
With my own self, and nobody beside,
How to effect the same: God helps not else.
'Tis I who, with my stock of craft and strength,
Choose the directer cut across the hedge,
Or keep the foot-track that respects a crop;
Lie down and rest; rise up and run; live spare;
Feed free, — all that's my business: but arrive,
Deliver message, bring the answer back,
And make my bow, I must; then God will speak, —
Praise me, or haply blame, as service proves.
To other men, to each and every one,
Another law: what likelier? God, perchance,
Grants each new man, by some as new a mode,
Intercommunication with himself,
Wreaking on finiteness infinitude;
By such a series of effects gives each

Last his own imprint: old, yet ever new,
The process: 'tis the way of Deity.
How it succeeds, he knows: I only know
That varied modes of creatureship abound,
Implying just as varied intercourse
For each with the Creator of them all.
Each has his own mind, and no other's mode.
What mode may yours be? I shall sympathize.
No doubt, you, good young lady that you are,
Despite a natural naughtiness or two,
Turn eyes up like a Pradier Magdalen,
And see an outspread providential hand
Above the owl's-wing aigrette—guard and guide—
Visibly o'er your path, about your bed,
Through all your practisings with London-town.
It points, you go; it stays fixed, and you stop:
You quicken its procedure by a word
Spoken, a thought in silence, prayer, and praise.
Well, I believe that such a hand may stoop,
And such appeals to it may stave off harm,
Pacify the grim guardian of this square,

And stand you in good stead on quarter-day:
Quite possible in your case, not in mine.
"Ah! but I choose to make the difference,
Find the emancipation?" No, I hope.
If I deceive myself, take noon for night,
Please to become determinedly blind
To the true ordinance of human life
Through mere presumption, that is my affair,
And truly a grave one: but as grave I think
Your affair, — yours, the specially observed;
Each favored person that perceives his path
Pointed him inch by inch, and looks above
For guidance, through the mazes of this world,
In what we call its meanest life-career, —
Not how to manage Europe properly,
But how keep open shop, and yet pay rent,
Rear household, and make both ends meet, — the same.
I say, such man is no less tasked than I
To duly take the path appointed him
By whatsoever sign he recognize.
Our insincerity on both our heads!

No matter what the object of a life,
Small work or large, — the making thrive a shop,
Or seeing that an empire take no harm, —
There are known fruits to judge obedience by.
You've read a ton's weight, now, of newspaper, —
Lives of me, gabble about the kind of prince:
You know my work i' the rough: I ask you, then,
Do I appear subordinated less
To hand-impulsion, one prime push for all,
Than little lives of men, the multitude
That cried out every quarter of an hour
For fresh instructions, did or did not work,
And praised in the odd minutes?

Eh, my dear?

Such is the reason why I acquiesced
In doing what seemed best for me to do,
So as to please myself on the great scale,
Having regard to immortality
No less than life; did that which head and heart
Prescribed my hand, in measure with its means
Of doing; used my special stock of power,

Not from the aforesaid head and heart alone,
But every sort of helpful circumstance,
Some problematic, and some nondescript;
All regulated by the single care
I' the last resort, — that I made thoroughly serve
The when and how, toiled where was need, reposed
As resolutely to the proper point,
Braved sorrow, courted joy, to just one end, —
Namely, that just the creature I was bound
To be I should become, nor thwart at all
God's purpose in creation. I conceive
No other duty possible to man, —
Highest mind, lowest mind, — no other law
By which to judge life failure or success,
What folks call being saved or cast away.

Such was my rule of life: I worked my best,
Subject to ultimate judgment, — God's, not man's.
Well, then, this settled, — take your tea, I beg,
And meditate the fact 'twixt sip and sip, —
This settled, — why I pleased myself, you saw,

By turning blot and blot into a line
O' the little scale, — we'll try now (as your tongue
Tries the concluding sugar-drop) what's meant
To please me most o' the great scale. Why, just now,
With nothing else to do within my reach,
Did I prefer making two blots one line
To making yet another separate
Third blot, and leaving those I found unlinked?
It meant, I like to use the thing I find,
Rather than strive at unfound novelty:
I make the best of the old, nor try for new.
Such will to act, such choice of action's way,
Constitute — when at work on the great scale,
Driven to their farthest natural consequence
By all the help from all the means — my own
Particular faculty of serving God,
Instinct for putting power to exercise
Upon some wish and want o' the time, I prove
Possible to mankind as best I may.
This constitutes my mission (grant the phrase):
Namely, to rule men, — men within my reach;

To order, influence, and dispose them so
As render solid, and stabilify
Mankind in particles, the light and loose,
For their good and my pleasure in the act.
Such good accomplished proves twice good to me, —
Good for its own sake, as the just and right;
And, in the effecting also, good again
To me its agent, tasked as suits my taste.

Is this much easy to be understood
At first glance? Now begin the steady gaze.

My rank (if I must tell you simple truth:
Telling were else not worth the whiff o' the weed
I lose for the tale's sake), dear, my rank i' the world,
Is hard to know and name precisely: err
I may, but scarcely over-estimate
My style and title. Do I class with men
Most useful to their fellows? Possibly,
Therefore, in some sort, best; but greatest mind
And rarest nature? Evidently no.

A conservator call me, if you please,
Not a creator nor destroyer, — one
Who keeps the world safe. I profess to trace
The broken circle of society;
Dim actual order I can redescribe,
Not only where some segment silver-true
Stays clear, but where the breaks of black commence,
Baffling you all who want the eye to probe,
As I make out yon problematic thin
White paring of your thumb-nail outside there,
Above the plaster monarch on his steed;
See an inch; name an ell; and prophesy
O' the rest that ought to follow, — the round moon
Now hiding in the night of things: that round,
I labor to demonstrate moon enough
For the month's purpose; that society,
Render efficient for the age's need:
Preserving you in either case the old,
Nor aiming at a new and greater thing, —
A sun for moon, a future to be made
By first abolishing the present law:

No such proud task for me by any means!
History shows you men whose master-touch
Not so much modifies as makes anew, —
Minds that transmute, nor need restore at all.
A breath of God made manifest in flesh
Subjects the world to change from time to time;
Alters the whole conditions of our race
Abruptly, not by unperceived degrees,
Nor play of elements already there,
But quite new leaven, leavening the lump,
And liker, so, the natural process. See!
Where Winter reigned for ages, — by a turn
I' the time, some star-change (ask geologists),
The ice-tracts split, clash, splinter, and disperse,
And there's an end of immobility,
Silence, and all that tinted pageant, base
To pinnacle, one flush from fairy-land
Dead-asleep and deserted somewhere, — see! —
As a fresh sun, wave, spring, and joy outburst.
Or else the earth it is, time starts from trance,
Her mountains tremble into fire, her plains

Heave blinded by confusion: what result?
New teeming growth, surprises of strange life
Impossible before, a world broke up
And re-made, order gained by law destroyed.
Not otherwise, in our society,
Follow like portents, all as absolute
Regenerations: they have birth at rare,
Uncertain, unexpected intervals
O' the world, by ministry impossible
Before and after fulness of the days:
Some dervis desert-spectre, swordsman, saint,
Law-giver, lyrist, — oh! we know the names.
Quite other these than I. Our time requires
No such strange potentate, — who else would dawn, —
No fresh force till the old have spent itself.
Such seems the natural economy.
To shoot a beam into the dark assists:
To make that beam do fuller service, spread
And utilize such bounty to the height, —
That assists also; and that work is mine.
I recognize, contemplate, and approve

The general compact of society,
Not simply as I see effected good,
But good i' the germ, each chance that's possible
I' the plan traced so far; all results, in short,
For better or worse of the operation due
To those exceptional natures, unlike mine,
Who, helping, thwarting, conscious, unaware,
Did somehow manage to so far describe
This diagram left ready to my hand,
Waiting my turn of trial. I see success,
See failure, see what makes or mars throughout.
How shall I else but help complete this plan,
Of which I know the purpose, and approve,
By letting stay therein what seems to stand,
And adding good thereto of easier reach
To-day than yesterday?

So much, no more!
Whereon, "No more than that?" inquire aggrieved
Half of my critics: "nothing new at all?
The old plan saved, instead of a sponged slate

And fresh-drawn figure?" While, "So much as that?"
Object their fellows of the other faith:
"Leave uneffaced the crazy labyrinth
Of alteration and amendment, lines
Which every dabster felt in duty bound
To signalize his power of pen and ink
By adding to a plan once plain enough?
Why keep each fool's bequeathment, scratch and blur
Which overscrawl and underscore the piece;
Nay, strengthen them by touches of your own?"

Well, that's my mission, so I serve the world,
Figure as man o' the moment, — in default
Of somebody inspired to strike such change
Into society, — from round to square,
The ellipsis to the rhomboid, — how you please,
As suits the size and shape o' the world he finds.
But this I can, — and nobody my peer, —
Do the best with the least change possible;
Carry the incompleteness on a stage;
Make what was crooked straight, and roughness smooth,

And weakness strong: wherein if I succeed,
It will not prove the worst achievement, sure,
In the eyes at least of one man, — one I look
Nowise to catch in critic company;
To wit, the man inspired, the genius' self,
Destined to come and change things thoroughly.
He, at least, finds his business simplified,
Distinguishes the done from undone, reads
Plainly what meant and did not mean this time
We live in, and I work on, and transmit
To such successor: he will operate
On good hard substance, not mere shade and shine.
Let all my critics, born to idleness
And impotency, get their good, and have
Their hooting at the giver: I am deaf,
Who find great good in this society,
Great gain, the purchase of great labor. Touch
The work I may and must, but — reverent
In every fall o' the finger-tip, no doubt.
Perhaps I find all good there's warrant for
I' the world as yet: nay, to the end of time;

Since evil never means part company
With mankind, only shift side and change shape.
I find advance i' the main, and notably
The Present an improvement on the Past,
And promise for the Future, which shall prove
Only the Present with its rough made smooth,
Its indistinctness emphasized: I hope
No better, nothing newer, for mankind,
But something equably smoothed everywhere, —
Good, reconciled with hardly-quite-as-good,
Instead of good and bad each jostling each.
"And that's all?" Ay, and quite enough for me!
We have toiled so long to gain what gain I find
I' the Present, let us keep it! We shall toil
So long before we gain, if gain God grant,
A Future with one touch of difference
I' the heart of things, and not their outside face,
Let us not risk the whiff of my cigar
For Fourier, Comte, and all that ends in smoke!

This I see clearest probably of men,

With power to act and influence, now alive:
Juster than they to the true state of things;
In consequence, more tolerant, that, side
By side, shall co-exist, and thrive alike
In the age, the various sorts of happiness
Moral, mark! — not material, — moods o' the mind
Suited to man and man his opposite:
Say, minor modes of movement, — hence to there,
Or thence to here, or simply round about, —
So long as each toe spares its neighbor's kibe,
Nor spoils the major march and main advance.
The love of peace, care for the family,
Contentment with what's bad, but might be worse, —
Good movements these! and good, too, discontent,
So long as that spurs good, which might be best,
Into becoming better anyhow:
Good, — pride of country, putting hearth and home
I' the background, out of undue prominence;
Good, — yearning after change, strife, victory,
And triumph. Each shall have its orbit marked,
But no more, — none impede the other's path

In this wide world; though each and all alike,
Save for me, fain would spread itself through space,
And leave its fellow not an inch of way.
I rule and regulate the course, excite,
Restrain; because the whole machine should march
Impelled by those diversely-moving parts,
Each blind to aught beside its little bent.
Out of the turnings round and round inside
Comes that straightforward world-advance I want,
And none of them supposes God wants too,
And gets through just their hinderance and my help.
I think that to have held the balance straight
For twenty years, say, weighing claim and claim,
And giving each its due, no less, no more, —
This was good service to humanity,
Right usage of my power in head and heart,
And reasonable piety beside.
Keep those three points in mind while judging me.
You stand, perhaps, for some one man, not men;
Represent this or the other interest,
Nor mind the general welfare; so, impugn

My practice, and dispute my value: why?
You man of faith, I did not tread the world
Into a paste, and thereof make a smooth
Uniform mound whereon to plant your flag,
The lily-white, above the blood and brains;
Nor yet did I, you man of faithlessness,
So roll things to the level which you love,
That you could stand at ease there, and survey
The universal Nothing undisgraced
By pert obtrusion of some old church-spire
I' the distance. Neither friend would I content;
Nor, as the world were simply meant for him,
Thrust out his fellow, and mend God's mistake.
Why, you two fools, — my dear friends all the same, —
Is it some change o' the world, and nothing else,
Contents you? Should whatever was, not be?
How thanklessly you view things! There's the root
Of the evil, source of the entire mistake:
You see no worth i' the world, nature, and life,
Unless we change what is to what may be;
Which means, — may be i' the brain of one of you!

"Reject what is?" — all capabilities, —
Nay, you may style them chances if you choose, —
All chances, then, of happiness that lie
Open to anybody that is born,
Tumbles into this life and out again, —
All that may happen, good and evil too,
I' the space between, to each adventurer
Upon this 'sixty, Anno Domini:
A life to live, — and such a life! a world
To learn, one's lifetime in, — and such a world!
How ever did the foolish pass for wise
By calling life a burden, man a fly
Or worm, or what's most insignificant?
"O littleness of man!" deplores the bard;
And then, for fear the Powers should punish him,
"O grandeur of the visible universe
Our human littleness contrasts withal!
O sun, O moon, ye mountains, and thou sea,
Thou emblem of immensity, thou this,
That, and the other! — what impertinence
In man to eat and drink and walk about,

And have his little notions of his own,
The while some wave sheds foam upon the shore!"
First of all, 'tis a lie some three times thick:
The bard,—this sort of speech being poetry,—
The bard puts mankind well outside himself,
And then begins instructing them: "This way
I and my friend the sea conceive of you!
What would you give to think such thoughts as ours
Of you and the sea together?" Down they go
On the humbled knees of them: at once they draw
Distinction, recognize no mate of theirs
In one, despite his mock humility,
So plain a match for what he plays with. Next
The turn of the great ocean-playfellow,
When the bard, leaving Bond Street very far
From ear-shot, cares not to ventriloquize,
But tells the sea its home-truths: "You, my match?
You, all this terror and immensity,
And what not? Shall I tell you what you are?
Just fit to hitch into a stanza: so
Wake up and set in motion who's asleep

O' the other side of you, in England, else
Unaware, as folk pace their Bond Street now,
Somebody here despises them so much !
Between us, — they are the ultimate ! to them
And their perception go these lordly thoughts :
Since what were ocean, — mane and tail to boot, —
Mused I not here, how make thoughts thinkable ?
Start forth my stanza, and astound the world !
Back, billows, to your insignificance !
Deep, you are done with ! "

Learn, my gifted friend,
There are two things i' the world, still wiser folk
Accept, — intelligence and sympathy.
You pant about unutterable power
I' the ocean, all you feel but cannot speak ?
Why, that's the plainest speech about it all :
You did not feel what was not to be felt.
Well, then, all else but what man feels is nought, —
The wash o' the liquor that o'erbrims the cup
Called man, and runs to waste adown his side,

Perhaps to feed a cataract: who cares?
I'll tell you: all the more I know mankind,
The more I thank God, like my grandmother,
For making me a little lower than
The angels, honor-clothed and glory-crowned.
This is the honor, — that no thing I know,
Feel, or conceive, but I can make my own
Somehow, by use of hand or head or heart:
This is the glory, — that in all conceived,
Or felt or known, I recognize a mind
Not mine, but like mine, — for the double joy, —
Making all things for me, and me for Him.
There's folly for you at this time of day!
So think it! and enjoy your ignorance
Of what — no matter for the worthy's name —
Wisdom set working in a noble heart,
When he, who was earth's best geometer
Up to that time of day, consigned his life
With its results into one matchless book, —
The triumph of the human mind so far,
All in geometry man yet could do, —

And then wrote on the dedication-page,
In place of name the universe applauds,
"But, God, what a geometer art thou!"
I suppose heaven is, through eternity,
The equalizing, ever and anon,
In momentary rapture, great with small,
Omniscience with intelligency, God
With man, — the thunder-glow from pole to pole
Abolishing, a blissful moment-space,
Great cloud alike and small cloud, in one fire, —
As sure to ebb as sure again to flow
When the new receptivity deserves
The new completion. There's the heaven for me.
And I say, therefore, to live out one's life
I' the world here, with the chance — whether by pain
Or pleasure be the process, long or short
The time, august or mean the circumstance
To human eye — of learning how set foot
Decidedly on some one path to heaven,
Touch one point in the circle whence all lines
Lead to the centre equally, — red lines

Or black lines, so they but produce themselves, —
This, I do say, — and here my sermon ends, —
This makes it worth our while to tenderly
Handle a state of things which mend we might,
Mar we may, but which meanwhile helps so far.
Therefore my end is, save society.

"And that's all?" twangs the never-railing taunt
O' the foe. "No novelty, creativeness,
Mark of the master that renews the age?"
"Nay, all that?" rather will demur my judge
I look to hear some day, — nor friend nor foe, —
"Did you attain, then, to perceive that God
Knew what he undertook when he made things?"
Ay: that my task was to co-operate
Rather than play the rival, chop and change
The order whence comes all the good we know,
With this, — good's last expression to our sense, —
That there's a further good conceivable
Beyond the utmost earth can realize;

And, therefore, that to change the agency,
The evil whereby good is brought about, —
Try to make good do good as evil does, —
Were just as if a chemist, wanting white,
And knowing black ingredients bred the dye,
Insisted these, too, should be white forsooth.
Correct the evil, mitigate your best,
Blend mild with harsh, and soften black to gray
If gray may follow with no detriment
To the eventual perfect purity;
But as for hazarding the main result
By hoping to anticipate one-half
In the intermediate process, — no, my friends!
This bad world I experience and approve:
Your good world, — with no pity, courage, hope,
Fear, sorrow, joy, devotedness, in short,
Which I account the ultimate of man,
Of which there's not one day nor hour but brings,
In flower or fruit, some sample of success
Out of this same society I save, —

None of it for me! That I might have none,
I rapped your tampering knuckles twenty years:
Such was the task imposed me, such my end.

Now for the means thereto. Ah, confidence!
Keep we together, or part company?
This is the critical minute. "Such my end?"
Certainly: how could it be otherwise?
Can there be question which was the right task,—
To save, or to destroy, society?
Why, even prove, that, by some miracle,
Destruction were the proper work to choose,
And that a torch best remedies what's wrong
I' the temple, whence the long procession wound
Of powers and beauties, earth's achievements all,—
The human strength that strove and overthrew;
The human love, that, weak itself, crowned strength;
The instinct, crying, "God is whence I came!"
The reason laying down the law, "And such
His will i' the world must be!" the leap and shout
Of genius, "For I hold his very thoughts,

The meaning of the mind of him!" nay, more,
The ingenuities; each active force,
That, turning in a circle on itself,
Looks neither up nor down, but keeps the spot,
Mere creature-like, and, for religion, works,
Works only and works ever, makes and shapes
And changes, still wrings more of good from less,
Still stamps some bad out where was worst before,
So leaves the handiwork, the act and deed,
Were it but house and land and wealth, to show
Here was a creature perfect in the kind,—
Whether as bee, beaver, or behemoth,
What's the importance? he has done his work
For work's sake, worked well, earned a creature's
praise,—
I say, concede that same fane, whence deploys,
Age after age, all this humanity,
Diverse but ever dear, out of the dark
Behind the altar into the broad day
By the portal; enter, and concede there mocks
Each lover of free motion and much space

A perplexed length of apse and aisle and nave, —
Pillared roof and carved screen, and what care I ? —
That irk the movement, and impede the march ;
Nay, possibly, bring flat upon his nose
At some odd break-neck angle, by some freak
Of old-world artistry, that personage,
Who, could he but have kept his skirts from grief,
And, catching at the hooks and crooks about,
Had stepped out on the daylight of our time
Plainly the man of the age, — still, still, I bar
Excessive conflagration in the case.
"Shake the flame freely!" shout the multitude :
The architect approves I stuck my torch
Inside a good stout lantern, hung its light
Above the hooks and crooks, and ended so.
To save society was well : the means
Whereby to save it, — there begins the doubt
Permitted you, imperative on me.
Were mine the best means ? Did I work aright
With powers appointed me ? since powers denied
Concern me nothing.

Well, my work, reviewed
Fairly, leaves more hope than discouragement.
First, there's the deed done: what I found I leave;
What tottered I kept stable: if it stand
One month without sustainment, still thank me,
The twenty years' sustainer! Now, observe,
Sustaining is no brilliant self-display,
Like knocking down, or even setting up.
Much bustle these necessitate; and still,
To vulgar eye, the mightier of the myth
Is Hercules, who substitutes his own
For Atlas' shoulder, and supports the globe
A whole day, — not the passive and obscure
Atlas who bore ere Hercules was born,
And is to go on bearing that same load
When Hercules turns ash on Œta's top.
'Tis the transition-stage, the tug and strain,
That strike men: standing still is stupid-like.
My pressure was too constant on the whole
For any part's eruption into space
'Mid sparkles, crackling, and much praise of me.

I saw, that, in the ordinary life,
Many of the little makes a mass of men
Important beyond greatness here and there;
As certainly as, in life exceptional,
When old things terminate, and new commence,
A solitary great man's worth the world.
God takes the business into his own hands
At such time: who creates the novel flower
Contrives to guard, and give it breathing-room:
I merely tend the corn-field, care for crop,
And weed no acre thin to let emerge
What prodigy may stifle there perchance;
No, though my eye have noted where he lurks.
Oh those mute myriads that spoke loud to me!—
The eyes that craved to see the light; the mouths
That sought the daily bread, and nothing more;
The hands that supplicated exercise;
Men that had wives, and women that had babes;
And all these making suit to only live!
Was I to turn aside from husbandry,
Leave hope of harvest for the corn, my care,

To play at horticulture, rear some rose
Or poppy into perfect leaf and bloom,
When, 'mid the furrows, up was pleased to sprout
Some man, cause, system, special interest
I ought to study, stop the world meanwhile?
"But I am liberty, philanthropy,
Enlightenment, or patriotism, the power
Whereby you are to stand or fall!" cries each:
"Mine, and mine only, be the flag you flaunt!"
And when I venture to object, "Meantime,
What of yon myriads with no flag at all,—
My crop, which who flaunts flag must tread across?"
"Now, this it is to have a puny mind!"
Admire my mental prodigies: "down, down,
Ever at home o' the level and the low,
There bides he brooding! Could he look above,
With less of the owl, and more of the eagle eye,
He'd see there's no way helps the little cause
Like the attainment of the great. Dare first
The chief emprise; dispel yon cloud between
The sun and us; nor fear, that, though our heads

Find earlier warmth and comfort from his ray,
What lies about our feet, the multitude,
Will fail of benefaction presently.
Come, now, let each of us a while cry truce
To special interests; make common cause
Against the adversary; or perchance
Mere dullard to his own plain interest!
Which of us will you choose? Since needs must be
Some one o' the warring causes you incline
To hold, i' the main, has right, and should prevail,
Why not adopt and give it prevalence?
Choose strict faith or lax incredulity, —
King, caste, and cultus, — or the rights of man,
Sovereignty of each Proudhon o'er himself,
And all that follows in just consequence;
Go free the stranger from a foreign yoke;
Or stay, concentrate energy at home;
Succeed! — when he deserves, the stranger will;
Comply with the great nation's impulse, print
By force of arms, — since reason pleads in vain,
And, 'mid the sweet compulsion, pity weeps, —

Hohenstiel-Schwangau on the universe!
Snub the Great Nation, cure the impulsive itch
With smartest fillip on a restless nose
Was ever launched by thumb and finger! Bid
Hohenstiel-Schwangau first repeal the tax
On pig-tails and pomatum, and then mind
Abstruser matters for next century!
Is your choice made? Why, then, act up to choice!
Leave the illogical touch, now here, now there,
I' the way of work; the tantalizing help
First to this, then the other opposite;
The blowing hot and cold, sham policy,
Sure ague of the mind, and nothing more,
Disease of the perception or the will,
That fain would hide in a fine name! Your choice;
Speak it out, and condemn yourself thereby!"

Well, Leicester Square is not the Residenz:
Instead of shrugging shoulder, turning friend
The deaf ear with a wink to the police,
I'll answer — by a question, wisdom's mode.

How many years, o' the average, do men
Live in this world? Some score, say computists.
Quintuple me that term, and give mankind
The likely hundred, and with all my heart
I'll take your task upon me, work your way,
Concentrate energy on some one cause;
Since, counsellor, I also have my cause,
My flag, my faith in its effect, my hope
In its eventful triumph for the good
O' the world. And once upon a time, when I
Was like all you, — mere voice, and nothing more, —
Myself took wings, soared sunward, and thence sang,
"Look where I live i' the loft! come up to me,
Groundlings, nor grovel longer! gain this height,
And prove you breathe here better than below!
Why, what emancipation far and wide
Will follow in a trice! They too can soar,
Each tenant of the earth's circumference
Claiming to elevate humanity;
They also must attain such altitude,
Live in the luminous circle that surrounds

The planet, not the leaden orb itself.
Press out, each point, from surface to yon verge
Which one has gained and guaranteed your realm!"
Ay, still my fragments wander, music-fraught,
Sighs of the soul, mine once, mine now, and mine
Forever! Crumbled arch, crushed aqueduct,
Alive with tremors in the shaggy growth
Of wildwood, crevice-sown, that triumphs there,
Imparting exultation to the hills!
Sweep of the swath when only the winds walk,
And waft my words above the grassy sea
Under the blinding blue that basks o'er Rome,—
Hear ye not still, "Be Italy again"?
And ye—what strikes the panic to your heart?
Decrepit council-chambers, where some lamp
Drives the unbroken black three paces off
From where the graybeards huddle in debate,
Dim cowls and capes, and midmost glimmers one
Like tarnished gold, and what they say is doubt,
And what they think is fear, and what suspends
The breath in them is not the plaster-patch

Time disengages from the painted wall
Where Raphael moulderingly bids adieu,
Nor tick of the insect turning tapestry
To dust, which a queen's finger traced of old;
But some word, resonant, redoubtable,
Of who once felt upon his head a hand
Whereof the head now apprehends his foot.
"Light in Rome, law in Rome, and liberty
O' the soul in Rome, — the free Church, the free State!
Stamp out the nature that's best typified
By its embodiment in Peter's dome,
The scorpion-body with the greedy pair
Of outstretched nippers, either colonnade
Agape for the advance of heads and hearts!"
There's one cause for you! — one, and only one;
For I am vocal through the universe,
I' the work-shop, manufactory, exchange
And market-place, seaport and custom-house,
O' the frontier: listen if the echoes die: —
"Unfettered commerce! Power to speak and hear,
And print and read! The universal vote!

Its rights for labor!" This, with much beside,
I spoke when I was voice, and nothing more,
But altogether such a one as you
My censors. "Voice, and nothing more, indeed!"
Re-echoes round me: "that's the censure; there's
Involved the ruin of you soon or late!
Voice, — when its promise beat the empty air;
And nothing more, — when solid earth's your stage,
And we desiderate performance, deed
For word, the realizing all you dreamed
In the old days: now, for deed, we find at door
O' the council-chamber posted, mute as mouse,
Hohenstiel-Schwangau, sentry and safeguard
O' the graybeards all a-chuckle, cowl to cape,
Who challenge Judas — that's endearment's style —
To stop their mouths, or let escape grimace,
While they keep cursing Italy and him.
The power to speak, hear, print, and read, is ours?
Ay, we learn where and how, when clapped inside
A convict-transport bound for cool Cayenne!
The universal vote we have; its urn

We also have, where votes drop, fingered o'er
By the universal prefect. Say, Trade's free,
And Toil turned master out o' the slave it was:
What then? These feed man's stomach; but his soul
Craves finer fare, nor lives by bread alone,
As somebody says somewhere. Hence you stand
Proved and recorded either false or weak,
Faulty in promise or performance: which?"
Neither, I hope. Once pedestalled on earth,
To act, not speak, I found earth was not air.
I saw that multitude of mine, and not
The nakedness and nullity of air,
Fit only for a voice to float in free.
Such eyes I saw that craved the light alone!
Such mouths that wanted bread, and nothing else!
Such hands that supplicated handiwork!
Men with the wives, and women with the babes;
Yet all these pleading just to live, not die!
Did I believe one whit less in belief,
Take truth for falsehood, wish the voice revoked
That told the truth to heaven for earth to hear?

No: this should be, and shall; but when and how?
At what expense to these who average
Your twenty years of life, my computists?
"Not bread alone," but bread before all else,
For these: the bodily want serve first, said I:
If earth-space and the lifetime help not here,
Where is the good of body having been?
But helping body, if we somewhat balk
The soul of finer fare, such food's to find
Elsewhere and afterward, — all indicates,
Even this selfsame fact, — that soul can starve,
Yet body still exist its twenty years:
While, stint the body, there's an end at once
O' the revel in the fancy that Rome's free,
And superstition's fettered, and one prints
Whate'er one pleases, and who pleases reads
The same, and speaks out, and is spoken to;
And divers hundred thousand fools may vote
A vote untampered with by one wise man,
And so elect Barabbas deputy
In lieu of his concurrent. I, who trace

The purpose written on the face of things
For my behoof and guidance (whoso needs
No such sustainment, sees beneath my signs,
Proves what I take for writing, penmanship,
Scribble, and flourish with no sense for me
O' the sort I solemnly go spelling out:
Let him! there's certain work of mine to show
Alongside his work; which gives warranty
Of shrewder vision in the workman, judge!), —
I, who trace Providence without a break
I' the plan of things, drop plumb on this plain print
Of an intention with a view to good,
That man is made in sympathy with man
At outset of existence, so to speak;
But in dissociation, more and more,
Man from his fellow, as their lives advance
In culture: still humanity, that's born
A mass, keeps flying off, fining away
Ever into a multitude of points,
And ends in isolation, each from each:
Peerless above i' the sky, the pinnacle;

Absolute contact, fusion, all below
At the base of being. How comes this about?—
This stamp of God, characterizing man,
And nothing else but man, in the universe, —
That while he feels with man (to use man's speech)
I' the little things of life, — its fleshly wants
Of food and rest and health and happiness,
Its simplest spirit-motions, loves and hates,
Hopes, fears, soul-cravings on the ignoblest scale,
O' the fellow-creature, — owns the bond at base, —
He tends to freedom and divergency
In the upward progress, plays the pinnacle
When life's at greatest? (grant again the phrase;
Because there's neither great nor small in life.)
"Consult thou for thy kind that have the eyes
To see, the mouths to eat, the hands to work,
Men with the wives, and women with the babes,"
Prompts Nature. "Care thou for thyself alone
I' the conduct of the mind God made thee with;
Think as if man had never thought before;
Act as if all creation hung attent

On the acting of such faculty as thine,
To take prime pattern from thy masterpiece."
Nature prompts also: neither law obeyed
To the uttermost by any heart and soul
We know or have in record; both of them
Acknowledged blindly by whatever man
We ever knew or heard of in this world.
"Will you have why and wherefore, and the fact
Made plain as pikestaff?" modern science asks.
"That mass man sprung from was a jelly-lump
Once on a time: he kept an after-course
Through fish and insect, reptile, bird, and beast,
Till he attained to be an ape at last,
Or last but one. And if this doctrine shock
In aught the natural pride"— Friend, banish fear,
The natural humility replies.
Do you suppose, even I, poor potentate,
Hohenstiel-Schwangau, who once ruled the roast,—
I was born able at all points to ply
My tools? or did I have to learn my trade?
Practise as exile ere perform as prince?

The world knows something of my ups and downs;
But grant me time, give me the management
And manufacture of a model me,—
Me fifty-fold, a prince without a flaw,—
Why, there's no social grade, the sordidest,
My embryo potentate should blink and 'scape.
King, all the better he was cobbler once,
He should know, sitting on the throne, how tastes
Life to who sweeps the doorway. But life's hard,
Occasion rare: you cut probation short,
And, being half instructed, on the stage
You shuffle through your part as best you may,
And bless your stars, as I do. God takes time.
I like the thought he should have lodged me once
I' the hole, the cave, the hut, the tenement,
The mansion, and the palace; made me learn
The feel o' the first, before I found myself
Loftier i' the last, not more emancipate:
From first to last of lodging, I was I,
And not at all the place that harbored me.
Do I refuse to follow farther yet

I' the backwardness; repine if tree and flower,
Mountain or streamlet, were my dwelling-place
Before I gained enlargement, grew mollusk?
As well account that way for many a thrill
Of kinship I confess to with the powers
Called Nature: animate, inanimate,
In parts or in the whole, there's something there
Man-like, that, somehow, meets the man in me.
My pulse goes altogether with the heart
O' the Persian, that old Xerxes, when he stayed
His march to conquest of the world, a day
I' the desert, for the sake of one superb
Plane-tree which queened it there in solitude;
Giving her neck its necklace, and each arm
Its armlet, suiting soft waist, snowy side,
With cincture and apparel. Yes, I lodged
In those successive tenements; perchance
Taste yet the straitness of them while I stretch
Limb, and enjoy new liberty the more.
And some abodes are lost or ruinous;
Some patched up and pieced out, and so transformed,

They still accommodate the traveller
His day of life-time. Oh! you count the links;
Descry no bar of the unbroken man?
Yes; and who welds a lump of ore, suppose
He likes to make a chain, and not a bar,
And reach by link on link, link small, link large,
Out to the due length, — why, there's forethought still
Outside o' the series, forging at one end;
While, at the other, there's — no matter what
The kind of critical intelligence
Believing that last link had last but one
For parent, and no link was, first of all,
Fitted to anvil, hammered into shape.
Else I accept the doctrine, and deduce
This duty, — that I recognize mankind
In all its height and depth, and length and breadth.
Mankind i' the main have little wants, not large:
I, being of will and power to help, i' the main,
Mankind, must help the least wants first. My friend,
That is, my foe, without such power and will,
May plausibly concentrate all he wields,

And do his best at helping some large want,
Exceptionally noble cause, that's seen
Subordinate enough from where I stand.
As he helps, I helped once, when like himself,
Unable to help better, work more wide;
And so would work with heart and hand to-day,
Did only computists confess a fault,
And multiply the single score by five, —
Five only, — give man's life its hundred years.
Change life, in me shall follow change to match.
Time were, then, to work here, there, everywhere,
By turns, and try experiment at ease!
Full time to mend as well as mar: why wait
The slow and sober uprise all around
O' the building? Let us run up, right to roof,
Some sudden marvel, piece of perfectness,
And testify what we intend the whole!
Is the world losing patience? "Wait!" say we:
"There's time: no generation needs to die
Unsolaced: you've a century in store!"
But no: I sadly let the voices wing

Their way i' the upper vacancy, nor test
Truth on this solid as I promised once.
Well, and what is there to be sad about?
The world's the world, life's life, and nothing else.
'Tis part of life, a property to prize,
That those o' the higher sort engaged i' the world
Should fancy they can change its ill to good,
Wrong to right, ugliness to beauty; find
Enough success in fancy turning fact
To keep the sanguine kind in countenance,
And justify the hope that busies them:
Failure enough, — to who can follow change
Beyond their vision; see new good prove ill
I' the consequence; see blacks and whites of life
Shift square indeed, but leave the checkered face
Unchanged i' the main, — failure enough for such
To bid ambition keep the whole from change
As their best service. I hope nought beside.
No, my brave thinkers, whom I recognize
Gladly, myself the first, as, in a sense,
All that our world's worth, flower and fruit of man!

Such minds myself award supremacy
Over the common insignificance,
When only Mind's in question: Body bows
To quite another government, you know.
Be Kant crowned king o' the castle in the air!
Hans Slouch — his own and children's mouths to feed
I' the hovel on the ground — wants meat, nor chews
"The Pure Critique of Reason" in exchange.
But, now, suppose I could allow your claims,
And quite change life to please you: would it please?
Would life comport with change, and still be life?
Ask, now, a doctor for a remedy:
There's his prescription. Bid him point you out
Which of the five or six ingredients saves
The sick man. "Such the efficacity?
Then why not dare and do things in one dose
Simple and pure, all virtue, no alloy
Of the idle drop and powder?" What's his word?
The efficacity, neat, were neutralized:
It wants dispersing and retarding; nay,
Is put upon its mettle, plays its part

Precisely through such hinderance everywhere,
Finds some mysterious give and take i' the case,
Some gain by opposition, he foregoes
Should he unfetter the medicament.
So with this thought of yours that fain would work
Free in the world: it wants just what it finds, —
The ignorance, stupidity, the hate,
Envy and malice and uncharitableness,
That bar your passage, break the flow of you
Down from those happy heights where many a cloud
Combined to give you birth, and bid you be
The royalest of rivers: on you glide
Silverly till you reach the summit-edge;
Then over, on to all that ignorance,
Stupidity, hate, envy, bluffs, and blocks,
Posted to fret you into foam and noise.
What of it? Up you mount in minute mist,
And bridge the chasm that crushed your quietude,
A spirit-rainbow, earth-born jewelry
Outsparkling the insipid firmament
Blue above Terni and its orange-trees.

Do not mistake me! You, too, have your rights.
Hans must not burn Kant's house above his head
Because he cannot understand Kant's book;
And still less must Hans' pastor burn Kant's self
Because Kant understands some books too well.
But, justice seen to on this little point,
Answer me, is it manly, is it sage,
To stop and struggle with arrangements here
It took so many lives, so much of toil,
To tinker up into efficiency?
Can't you contrive to operate at once —
Since time is short, and art is long — to show
Your quality i' the world, whate'er you boast,
Without this fractious call on folks to crush
The world together just to set you free,
Admire the capers you will cut perchance,
Nor mind the mischief to your neighbors?

"Age!
Age and experience, bring discouragement,"
You taunt me: I maintain the opposite.

Am I discouraged, who — perceiving health,
Strength, beauty, as they tempt the eye of soul,
Are uncombinable with flesh and blood —
Resolve to let my body live its best,
And leave my soul what better yet may be,
Or not be, in this life or afterward? —
In either fortune, wiser than who waits
Till magic art procure a miracle.
In virtue of my very confidence
Mankind ought to outgrow its babyhood,
I prescribe rocking, deprecate rough hands,
While thus the cradle holds it past mistake.
Indeed, my task's the harder, — equable
Sustainment everywhere, all strain, no push, —
Whereby friends credit me with indolence,
Apathy, hesitation. "Stand stock-still
If able to move briskly? 'All a-strain,' —
So must we compliment your passiveness?
Sound asleep, rather!"

Just the judgment passed

Upon a statue, luckless like myself,
I saw at Rome once! 'Twas some artist's whim
To cover all the accessories close
I' the group, and leave you only Laocoön,
With neither sons nor serpents to denote
The purpose of his gesture. Then a crowd
Was called to try the question; criticise
Wherefore such energy of legs and arms,
Nay, eyeballs starting from the socket. One, —
I give him leave to write my history, —
Only one, said, "I think the gesture strives
Against some obstacle we cannot see."
All the rest made their minds up: "'Tis a yawn
Of sheer fatigue subsiding to repose;
The statue's 'Somnolency' clear enough!"

There, my arch stranger-friend, my audience both
And arbitress, you have one-half your wish,
At least, — you know the thing I tried to do
All, so far, to my praise and glory; all
Told as befits the self-apologist,

Who ever promises a candid sweep
And clearance of those errors, miscalled crimes,
None knows more, none laments so much, as he,
And ever rises from confession, proved
A god whose fault was — trying to be man.
Just so, fair judge, — if I read smile aright, —
I condescend to figure in your eyes
As biggest heart and best of Europe's friends,
And hence my failure. God will estimate
Success one day; and, in the mean time, — you!

I dare say there's some fancy of the sort
Frolicking round this final puff I send
To die up yonder in the ceiling-rose, —
Some consolation-stakes, we losers win!
A plague of the return to "I — I — I
Did this, meant that, hoped, feared, the other thing!"
Autobiography, adieu! The rest
Shall make amends, be pure blame, history
And falsehood; not the ineffective truth,
But Thiers-and-Victor-Hugo exercise.

Hear what I never was, but might have been
I' the better world where goes tobacco-smoke!
Here lie the dozen volumes of my life:
(Did I say "lie"? the pregnant word will serve.)
Cut on to the concluding chapter, though;
Because the little hours begin to strike.
Hurry Thiers-Hugo to the labor's end!

Something like this the unwritten chapter reads.

Exemplify the situation thus!
Hohenstiel-Schwangau, being, no dispute,
Absolute mistress, chose the Assembly, first,
To serve her; chose this man, its president
Afterward, to serve also, — specially
To see that they did service one and all.
And now the proper term of years was out
When the head servant must vacate his place;
And nothing lay so patent to the world
As that his fellow-servants one and all
Were — mildly make we mention — knaves or fools,

Each of them with his purpose flourished full
I' the face of you by word and impudence,
Or filtered slyly out by nod and wink,
And nudge upon your sympathetic rib;
That not one minute more did knave or fool
Mean to keep faith, and serve as he had sworn
Hohenstiel-Schwangau, once that head away.
Why did such swear, except to get the chance,
When time should ripen and confusion bloom,
Of putting Hohenstielers-Schwangauese
To the true use of human property?
Restoring souls and bodies, — this to pope,
And that to king, that other to his planned
Perfection of a share-and-share-alike,
That other still to empire absolute
In shape of the head servant's very self
Transformed to master whole and sole: each scheme
Discussible, concede one circumstance, —
That each scheme's parent were, beside himself,
Hohenstiel-Schwangau, not her serving-man
Sworn to do service in the way she chose

Rather than his way, — way superlative,
Only — by some infatuation — his
And his and his, and every one's but hers
Who stuck to just the Assembly and the head.
I make no doubt the head, too, had his dream
Of doing sudden duty swift and sure
On all that heap of untrustworthiness;
Catching each vaunter of the villany
He meant to perpetrate when time was ripe,
Once the head servant fairly out of doors;
And caging here a knave, and there a fool,
Cry, "Mistress of the servants, these and me,
Hohenstiel-Schwangau! I, their trusty head,
Pounce on a pretty scheme concocting here,
That's stopped, extinguished, by my vigilance.
Your property is safe again; but mark!
Safe in these hands, not yours, who lavish trust
Too lightly. Leave my hands their charge a while!
I know your business better than yourself:
Let me alone about it! Some fine day,
Once we are rid of the embarrassment,

You shall look up and see your longings crowned!"
Such fancy may have tempted to be false;
But this man chose truth, and was wiser so.
He recognized, that, for great minds i' the world,
There is no trial like the appropriate one
Of leaving little minds their liberty
Of littleness to blunder on through life;
Now aiming at right end by foolish means,
Now at absurd achievement through the aid
Of good and wise means,—trial to acquiesce
In folly's life-long privilege, though with power
To do the little minds the good they need,
Despite themselves, by just abolishing
Their right to play the part and fill the place
I' the scheme of things He schemed who made alike
Great minds and little minds, saw use for each.
Could the orb sweep those puny particles
It just half-lights at distance, hardly leads
I' the leash; sweep out each speck of them from space
They anticise in with their days and nights
And whirlings round and dancings off, forsooth,

And all that fruitless individual life
One cannot lend a beam to but they spoil;
Sweep them into itself, and so, one star,
Preponderate henceforth i' the heritage
Of heaven! No! in less senatorial phrase,
The man endured to help, not save outright,
The multitude, by substituting him
For them, his knowledge, will, and way, for God's;
Not change the world, such as it is, and was,
And will be, for some other, suiting all
Except the purpose of the Maker. No!
He saw that weakness, wickedness, will be,
And therefore should be; that the perfect man,
As we account perfection, — at most pure
O' the special gold, whate'er the form it take,
Head-work or heart-work, fined and thrice-refined
I' the crucible of life, whereto the powers
Of the refiner, one and all, were flung
To feed the flame their utmost, — e'en that block,
He holds out breathlessly triumphant, — breaks
Into some poisonous ore, its opposite,

At the very purest, so compensating
The Adversary — what if we believe? —
For earlier stern exclusion of his stuff.
See the sage, with the hunger for the truth,
And see his system that's all true, except
The one weak place that's stanchioned by a lie!
The moralist, that walks with head erect
I' the crystal charity of air so long,
Until a stumble, and the man's one mire!
Philanthropy undoes the social knot
With axe-edge; makes love room 'twixt head and trunk!
Religion — but enough: the thing's too clear!
Well, if these sparks break out i' the greenest tree,
Our topmost of performance, yours and mine,
What will be done i' the dry ineptitude
Of ordinary mankind, bark and bole,
All seems ashamed of but their mother-earth?
Therefore throughout his term of servitude
He did the appointed service, and forbore
Extraneous action that were duty else,
Done by some other servant, idle now

Or mischievous: no matter, each his own, —
Own task, and, in the end, own praise or blame!
He suffered them strut, prate, and brag their best;
Squabble at odds on every point save one,
And there shake hands; agree to trifle time;
Obstruct advance with, each, his cricket-cry,
"Wait till the head be off the shoulders here!
Then comes my king, my pope, my autocrat,
My socialist republic to her own, —
To wit, that property of only me,
Hohenstiel-Schwangau, who conceits herself
Free, forsooth, and expects I keep her so!" —
Nay, suffered when, perceiving with dismay
His silence paid no tribute to that noise,
They turned on him. "Dumb menace in that mouth,
Malice in that unstridulosity!
He cannot but intend some stroke of state
Shall signalize his passage into peace
Out of the creaking; hinder transference
O' the Hohenstielers-Schwangauese to king,
Pope, autocrat, or socialist republic! That's

Exact the cause his lips unlocked would cry!
Therefore be stirring; brave, beard, bully him!
Dock, by the million, of its friendly joints,
The electoral body short at once! who did
May do again, and undo us beside.
Wrest from his hands the sword for self-defence,
The right to parry any thrust in play
We peradventure please to meditate!"
And so forth; creak, creak, creak: and ne'er a line
His locked mouth oped the wider, till at last,
O' the long degraded and insulting day,
Sudden the clock told it was judgment-time.
Then he addressed himself to speak indeed
To the fools, not knaves: they saw him walk straight down
Each step of the eminence, as he first engaged,
And stand at last o' the level, — all he swore.
"People, and not the people's varletry, —
This is the task you set myself and these!
Thus I performed my part of it, and thus
They thwarted me throughout, here, here, and here:

Study each instance! yours the loss, not mine.
What they intend now is demonstrable
As plainly: here's such man; and here's such mode
Of making you some other than the thing
You, wisely or unwisely, choose to be,
And only set him up to keep you so.
Do you approve this? Yours the loss, not mine.
Do you condemn it? There's a remedy.
Take me, — who know your mind, and mean your good,
With clearer head and stouter arm than they,
Or you, or, haply, anybody else, —
And make me master for the moment! Choose
What time, what power you trust me with: I, too,
Will choose as frankly ere I trust myself
With time and power: they must be adequate
To the end and aim, since mine the loss, with yours,
If means be wanting: once their worth approved,
Grant them, and I shall forthwith operate —
Ponder it well! — to the extremest stretch
O' the power you trust me; if with unsuccess,
God wills it, and there's nobody to blame."

Whereon the people answered with a shout,
"The trusty one! no tricksters any more!"
How could they other? He was in his place.

What followed? Just what he foresaw, what proved
The soundness of both judgments, — his, o' the knaves
And fools, each trickster with his dupe; and theirs,
The people, in what head and arm should help.
There was uprising, masks dropped, flags unfurled,
Weapons outflourished in the wind, my faith!
Heavily did he let his fist fall plumb
On each perturber of the public peace,
No matter whose the wagging head it broke, —
From bald-pate craft and greed and impudence
Of night-hawk at first chance to prowl and prey
For glory and a little gain beside,
Passing for eagle in the dusk of the age,
To florid head-top, foamy patriotism,
And tribunitial daring, breast laid bare
Through confidence in rectitude, with hand
On private pistol in the pocket: these,

And all the dupes of these, who lent themselves
As dust and feather do to help offence
O' the wind that whirls them at you, then subsides
In safety somewhere, leaving filth afloat,
Annoyance you may brush from eyes and beard, —
These he stopped ; bade the wind's spite howl or whine
Its worst outside the building, wind conceives
Meant to be pulled together, and become
Its natural playground so. What foolishness
Of dust or feather proved importunate,
And fell 'twixt thumb and finger, found them gripe
To detriment of bulk and buoyancy.
Then followed silence and submission. Next
The inevitable comment came on work
And work's cost : he was censured as profuse
Of human life and liberty ; too swift
And thorough his procedure, who had lagged
At the outset, lost the opportunity
Through timid scruples as to right and wrong.
"There's no such certain mark of a small mind"
(So did Sagacity explain the fault)

"As when it needs must square away, and sink
To its own small dimensions, private scale
Of right and wrong, — humanity i' the large,
The right and wrong of the universe, forsooth!
This man addressed himself to guard and guide
Hohenstiel-Schwangau. When the case demands
He frustrate villany in the egg, unhatched,
With easy stamp and minimum of pang
E'en to the punished reptile, 'There's my oath
Restrains my foot,' objects our guide and guard;
'I must leave guardianship and guidance now:
Rather than stretch one handbreath of the law,
I am bound to see it break from end to end.
First show me death i' the body politic;
Then prescribe pill and potion, what may please
Hohenstiel-Schwangau! all is for her sake:
'Twas she ordained my service should be so.
What if the event demonstrāte her unwise,
If she unwill the thing she willed before?
I hold to the letter, and obey the bond,
And leave her to perdition loyally.'

Whence followed thrice the expenditure we blame
Of human life and liberty: for want
O' the by-blow came deliberate butcher's-work!"
"Elsewhere go carry your complaint," bade he.
"Least, largest, there's one law for all the minds,
Here or above: be true at any price!
'Tis just o' the great scale that such happy stroke
Of falsehood would be found a failure. Truth
Still stands unshaken at her base by me,
Reigns paramount i' the world, for the large good
O' the long late generations, — I and you
Forgotten like this buried foolishness!
Not so the good I rooted in its grave."

This is why he refused to break his oath;
Rather appealed to the people; gained the power
To act as he thought best; then used it once
For all, no matter what the consequence
To knaves and fools. As thus began his sway,
So, through its twenty years, one rule of right
Sufficed him: govern for the many first,

The poor mean multitude, all mouths and eyes;
Bid the few, better favored in the brain,
Be patient, nor presume on privilege,
Help him, or else be quiet, — never crave
That he help them, — increase, forsooth, the gulf
Yawning so terribly 'twixt mind and mind
I' the world here, which his purpose was to block
At bottom, were it by an inch, and bridge,
If by a filament, no more, at top.
Equalize things a little! And the way
He took to work that purpose out was plain
Enough to intellect and honesty
And — superstition style it if you please,
So long as you allow there was no lack
O' the quality imperative in man —
Reverence. You see deeper? thus saw he,
And, by the light he saw, must walk: how else
Was he to do his part? the man's, with might
And main, and not a faintest touch of fear,
Sure he was in the hand of God, who comes
Before and after, with a work to do

Which no man helps nor hinders. Thus the man, —
So timid when the business was to touch
The uncertain order of humanity,
Imperil, for a problematic cure
Of grievance on the surface, any good
I' the deep of things, dim yet discernible, —
This same man, so irresolute before,
Show him a true excrescence to cut sheer,
A devil's-graft on God's foundation-stone,
Then — no complaint of indecision more!
He wrenched out the whole canker, root and branch,
Deaf to who cried the world would tumble in
At its four corners if he touched a twig.
Witness that lie of lies, arch-infamy,
When the Republic, with all life involved
In just this law, — "Each people rules itself
Its own way, not as any stranger please," —
Turned, and, for first proof she was living, bade
Hohenstiel-Schwangau fasten on the throat
Of the first neighbor that claimed benefit
O' the law herself established: "Hohenstiel

For Hohenstielers! Rome, by parity
Of reasoning, for Romans? That's a jest
Wants proper treatment, — lancet-puncture suits
The proud flesh: Rome ape Hohenstiel forsooth!"
And so the siege and slaughter and success,
Whereof we nothing doubt that Hohenstiel
Will have to pay the price in God's good time;
Which does not always fall on Saturday,
When the world looks for wages. Anyhow,
He found this infamy triumphant. Well,
Sagacity suggested, make this speech: —
"The work was none of mine: suppose wrong wait,
Stand over for redressing? Mine for me;
My predecessors' work on their own head!
Meantime, there's plain advantage, should we leave
Things as we find them. Keep Rome manacled
Hand and foot: no fear of unruliness!
Her foes consent to even seem our friends
So long, no longer. Then there's glory got
I' the boldness and bravado to the world.
The disconcerted world must grin and bear

The old saucy writing,—'Grunt thereat who may:
So shall things be, for such my pleasure is,—
Hohenstiel-Schwangau.' How that reads in Rome,
I' the capitol where Brennus broke his pate!
And what a flourish for our journalists!"
Only it was nor read nor flourished of,
Since not a moment did such glory stay
Excision of the canker! Out it came,
Root and branch, with much roaring, and some blood,
And plentiful abuse of him from friend
And foe. Who cared? Not Nature, that assuaged
The pain, and set the patient on his legs
Promptly: the better!—had it been the worse,
'Tis Nature you must try conclusions with,
Not he; since nursing canker kills the sick
For certain, while to cut may cure at least.
"Ah," groaned a second time Sagacity,
"Again the little mind, precipitate,
Rash, rude, when even in the right, as here!
The great mind knows the power of gentleness;
Only tries force because persuasion fails.

Had this man, by prelusive trumpet-blast,
Signified, 'Truth and Justice mean to come;
Nay, fast approach your threshold! Ere they knock,
See that the house be set in order, swept
And garnished, windows shut, and doors thrown wide.
The free State comes to visit the free Church:
Receive her! or — or — never mind what else!'
Thus moral suasion heralding brute force,
How had he seen the old abuses die,
And new life kindle here, there, everywhere,
Roused simply by that mild yet potent spell, —
Beyond or beat of drum, or stroke of sword, —
Public opinion!"

"How, indeed?" he asked,
"When all to see, after some twenty years,
Were your own fool-face waiting for the sight,
Faced by as wide a grin from ear to ear
O' the knaves, that, while the fools were waiting, worked,
Broke yet another generation's heart, —
Twenty years' respite helping! Teach your nurse

'Compliance with, before you suck, the teat!'
Find what that means, and meanwhile hold your tongue!"

Whereof the war came which he knew must be.

Now, this had proved the dry-rot of the race
He ruled o'er, that in the old day, when was need
They fought for their own liberty and life,
Well did they fight, none better: whence such love
Of fighting somehow still for fighting's sake
Against no matter whose the liberty
And life, so long as self-conceit should crow
And clap the wing, while Justice sheathed her claw,—
That what had been the glory of the world,
When thereby came the world's good, grew its plague
Now that the champion-armor, donned to dare
The dragon once, was clattered up and down
Highway and by-path of the world at peace,
Merely to mask marauding, or for sake
O' the shine and rattle that apprised the fields

Hohenstiel-Schwangau was a fighter yet,
And would be till the weary world suppressed
A peccant humor out of fashion now.
Accordingly, the world spoke plain at last;
Promised to punish who next played with arms.

So at his advent, such discomfiture
Taking its true shape of beneficence,
Hohenstiel-Schwangau, half sad and part wise,
Sat: if with wistful eye reverting oft
To each pet weapon rusty on its peg,
Yet with a sigh of satisfaction too,
That, peacefulness become the law, herself
Got the due share of godsends in its train,
Cried shame, and took advantage quietly.
Still, so the dry-rot had been nursed into
Blood, bones, and marrow, that, from worst to best,
All, — clearest brains and soundest hearts, save here,
All had this lie acceptable for law
Plain as the sun at noonday, — "War is best,
Peace is worst; peace we only tolerate

As needful preparation for new war:
War may be for whatever end we will;
Peace only as the proper help thereto.
Such is the law of right and wrong for us,
Hohenstiel-Schwangau; for the other world,
As naturally, quite another law.
Are we content? — the world is satisfied.
Discontent? — then the world must give us leave
Strike right and left to exercise our arm,
Torpid of late, through overmuch repose,
And show its strength is still superlative
At somebody's expense in life or limb:
Which done, let peace succeed, and last a year!"
Such devil's-doctrine was so judged God's law,
We say, when this man stepped upon the stage,
That it had seemed a venial fault at most
Had he once more obeyed Sagacity.
"You come i' the happy interval of peace,
The favorable weariness from war:
Prolong it! — artfully, as if intent
On ending peace as soon as possible.

Quietly so increase the sweets of ease
And safety, so employ the multitude,
Put hod and trowel so in idle hands,
So stuff and stop the wagging jaws with bread,
That Selfishness shall surreptitiously
Do Wisdom's office; whisper in the ear
Of Hohenstiel-Schwangau, there's a pleasant feel
In being gently forced down, pinioned fast
To the easy arm-chair by the pleading arms
O' the world beseeching her to there abide
Content with all the harm done hitherto,
And let herself be petted in return,
Free to re-wage, in speech and prose and verse,
The old unjust wars, nay, — in verse and prose
And speech, — to vaunt new victories, as vile
A plague o' the future, — so that words suffice
For present comfort, and no deeds denote
That — tired of illimitable line on line
Of boulevard-building, tired o' the theatre
With the tuneful thousand in their thrones above,
For glory of the male intelligence,

And Nakedness in her due niche below,
For illustration of the female use —
She, 'twixt a yawn and sigh, prepares to slip
Out of the arm-chair, wants some blood again
From over the boundary to color up
The sheeny sameness, keep the world aware
Hohenstiel-Schwangau must have exercise
Despite the petting of the universe!
Come, you're a city-builder: what's the way
Wisdom takes, when time needs that she entice
Some fierce tribe, castled on the mountain-peak,
Into the quiet and amenity
O' the meadow-land below? By crying, 'Done
With fight now, down with fortress'? Rather, 'Dare
On, dare ever, not a stone displaced!'
Cries Wisdom, 'Cradle of our ancestors,
Be bulwark; give our children safety still!
Who of our children please may stoop and taste
O' the valley-fatness, unafraid; for why?
At first alarm, they have thy mother-ribs
To run upon for refuge: foes forget

Scarcely what Terror on her vantage-coigne,
Couchant supreme among the powers of air,
Watches — prepared to pounce — the country wide!
Meanwhile the encouraged valley holds its own,
From the first hut's adventure in descent,
Half home, half hiding-place, to dome and spire
Befitting the assured metropolis:
Nor means offence to the fort which caps the crag,
All undismantled of a turret-stone,
And bears the banner-pole that creaks at times,
Embarrassed by the old emblazonment,
When festal days are to commemorate.
Otherwise left untenanted, no doubt,
Since, never fear, our myriads from below
Would rush, if needs were, man the walls once more,
Renew the exploits of the earlier time
At moment's notice! But, till notice sound,
Inhabit we in ease and opulence!'
And so, till one day thus a notice sounds,
Not trumpeted, but in a whisper-gust
Fitfully playing through mute city streets

At midnight weary of day's feast and game, —
'Friends, your famed fort's a ruin past repair!
Its use is, to proclaim it had a use
Stolen away long since. Climb to study there
How to paint barbican and battlement
I' the scenes of our new theatre! We fight
Now — by forbidding neighbors to sell steel
Or buy wine, not by blowing out their brains!
Moreover, while we let time sap the strength
O' the walls omnipotent in menace once,
Neighbors would seem to have prepared surprise;
Run up defences in a mushroom growth,
For all the world like what we boasted: brief, —
Hohenstiel-Schwangau's policy is peace!'"

Ay, so Sagacity advised him filch
Folly from fools; handsomely substitute
The dagger o' lath, while gay they sang and danced
For that long dangerous sword they liked to feel,
Even at feast-time, clink and make friends start.
No! he said, "Hear the truth, and bear the truth,

And bring the truth to bear on all you are
And do, assured that only good comes thence,
Whate'er the shape good take! While I have rule,
Understand! — war for war's sake, war for the sake
O' the good war gets you as war's sole excuse,
Is damnable, and damned shall be. You want
Glory? Why, so do I, and so does God.
Where is it found, — in this paraded shame, —
One particle of glory? Once you warred
For liberty against the world, and won:
There was the glory. Now you fain would war
Because the neighbor prospers overmuch;
Because there has been silence half an hour,
Like heaven on earth, without a cannon-shot
Announcing Hohenstielers-Schwangauese
Are minded to disturb the jubilee;
Because the loud tradition echoes faint,
And who knows but posterity may doubt
If the great deeds were ever done at all,
Much less believe, were such to do again,
So the event would follow: therefore prove

The old power at the expense of somebody!
O Glory!—gilded bubble, bard and sage
So nickname rightly,—would thy dance endure
One moment, would thy mocking make believe
Only one upturned eye thy ball was gold,
Hadst thou less breath to buoy thy vacancy
Than a whole multitude expends in praise,
Less range for roaming than from head to head
Of a whole people? Flit, fall, fly again;
Only fix never where the resolute hand
May prick thee, prove the lie thou art, at once!
Give me real intellect to reason with,
No multitude, no entity that apes
One wise man, being but a million fools!
How and whence wishest glory, thou wise one?
Wouldst get it—didst thyself guide Providence—
By stinting of his due each neighbor round
In strength and knowledge and dexterity,
So as to have thy littleness grow large
By all those somethings once, turned nothings now,
As children make a molehill mountainous

By scooping out the plain into a trench,
And saving so their favorite from approach?
Quite otherwise the cheery game of life,
True yet mimetic warfare, whereby man
Does his best with his utmost, and so ends
The victor most of all in fair defeat.
Who thinks, — would he have no one think beside?
Who knows, who does, — must other learning die,
And action perish? Why, our giant proves
No better than a dwarf, with rivalry
Prostrate around him. 'Let the whole race stand
And try conclusions fairly!' he cries first.
Show me the great man would engage his peer
Rather by grinning, 'Cheat, thy gold is brass!'
Than granting, 'Perfect piece of purest ore!
Still is it less good mintage, this of mine?'
Well, and these right and sound results of soul
I' the strong and healthy one wise man, — shall such
Be vainly sought for, scornfully renounced
I' the multitude that make the entity, —
The people? — to what purpose, if no less,

In power and purity of soul, below
The reach of the unit than in multiplied
Might of the body, vulgarized the more,
Above, in thick and threefold brutishness?
See! you accept such one wise man, myself:
Wiser or less wise, still I operate
From my own stock of wisdom, nor exact
Of other sort of natures you admire,
That whoso rhymes a sonnet pays a tax,
Who paints a landscape dips brush at his cost,
Who scores a septet true for strings and wind
Mulcted must be: else how should I impose
Properly, attitudinize aright,
Did such conflicting claims as these divert
Hohenstiel-Schwangau from observing me?
Therefore what I find facile, you be sure,
With effort or without it, you shall dare, —
You, I aspire to make my better self,
And truly the Great Nation. No more war
For war's sake, then! and — seeing wickedness
Springs out of folly — no more foolish dread

O' the neighbor waxing too inordinate
A rival through his gain of wealth and ease!
What?—keep me patient, Powers!—the people here,
Earth presses to her heart, nor owns a pride
Above her pride i' the race all flame and air
And aspiration to the boundless Great,
The incommensurably Beautiful,
Whose very falterings groundward come of flight
Urged by a pinion all too passionate
For heaven and what it holds of gloom and glow:
Bravest of thinkers, bravest of the brave
Doers, exalt in science, rapturous
In art, the—more than all—magnetic race
To fascinate their fellows, mould mankind
Hohenstiel-Schwangau-fashion,—these, what?—these
Will have to abdicate their primacy
Should such a nation sell them steel untaxed,
And such another take itself, on hire
For the natural sen'night, somebody for lord
Unpatronized by me whose back was turned?
Or such another yet would fain build bridge,

Lay rail, drive tunnel, busy its poor self
With its appropriate fancy: so there's — flash —
Hohenstiel-Schwangau up in arms at once!
Genius has somewhat of the infantine;
But of the childish not a touch nor taint,
Except through self-will, which, being foolishness,
Is certain, soon or late, of punishment.
Which Providence avert! — and, that it may
Avert what both of us would so deserve,
No foolish dread o' the neighbor, I enjoin!
By consequence, no wicked war with him,
While I rule!

Does that mean — no war at all
When just the wickedness I here proscribe
Comes, haply, from the neighbor? Does my speech
Precede the praying that you beat the sword
To plough-share, and the spear to pruning-hook,
And sit down henceforth under your own vine
And fig-tree through the sleepy summer month,
Letting what hurly-burly please explode

On the other side the mountain-frontier? No,
Beloved! I foresee and I announce
Necessity of warfare in one case,
For one cause: one way, I bid broach the blood
O' the world. For truth and right, and only right
And truth, — right, truth, on the absolute scale of God,
No pettiness of man's admeasurement, —
In such case only, and for such one cause,
Fight your hearts out, whatever fate betide
Hands energetic to the uttermost!
Lie not! Endure no lie which needs your heart
And hand to push it out of mankind's path;
No lie that lets the natural forces work
Too long ere lay it plain and pulverized,
Seeing man's life lasts only twenty years!
And such a lie, before both man and God,
Being, at this time present, Austria's rule
O'er Italy, — for Austria's sake the first,
Italy's next, and our sake last of all,
Come with me and deliver Italy!
Smite hip and thigh until the oppressor leave

Free from the Adriatic to the Alps
The oppressed one! We were they who laid her low
In the old bad day when Villany braved Truth
And Right, and laughed, 'Henceforward, God deposed,
The Devil is to rule forevermore
I' the world!' — whereof to stop the consequence,
And for atonement of false glory there
Gaped at and gabbled over by the world,
We purpose to get God enthroned again
For what the world will gird at as sheer shame
I' the cost of blood and treasure. 'All for nought, —
Not even, say, some patch of province, splice
O' the frontier? — some snug honorarium-fee
Shut into glove and pocketed apace?'
(Questions Sagacity) 'in deference
To the natural susceptibility
Of folks at home, unwitting of that pitch
You soar to, and misdoubting if Truth, Right,
And the other such augustnesses, repay
Expenditure in coin o' the realm, but prompt
To recognize the cession of Savoy

And Nice as marketable value!' No,
Sagacity! go preach to Metternich,
And, sermon ended, stay where he resides!
Hohenstiel-Schwangau, you and I must march
The other road! war for the hate of war,
Not love, this once!" So Italy was free.

What else noteworthy and commendable
I' the man's career?—that he was resolute
No trepidation, much less treachery,
On his part, should imperil from its poise
The ball o' the world, heaved up at such expense
Of pains so far, and ready to rebound,
Let but a finger maladroitly fall
Under pretence of making fast and sure
The inch gained by late volubility,
And run itself back to the ancient rest
At foot o' the mountain. Thus he ruled, gave proof
The world had gained a point, progressive so,
By choice, this time, as will and power concurred,
O' the fittest man to rule; not chance of birth,

Or such-like dice-throw. Oft Sagacity
Was at his ear: "Confirm this clear advance;
Support this wise procedure! You, elect
O' the people, mean to justify their choice,
And out-king all the kingly imbeciles.
But that's just half the enterprise: remains
You find them a successor like yourself
In head and heart and eye and hand and aim,
Or all done's undone; and whom hope to mould
So like you as the pupil Nature sends,
The son and heir's completeness which you lack?
Lack it no longer! Wed the pick o' the world
Where'er you think you find it! Should she be
A queen, — tell Hohenstielers-Schwangauese,
'So do the old enthroned decrepitudes
Acknowledge, in the rotten hearts of them,
Their knell is knolled, they hasten to make peace
With the new order, recognize in me
Your right to constitute what king you will,
Cringe therefore crown in hand, and bride on arm,
To both of us: we triumph, I suppose!'

Is it the other sort of rank? — bright eye,
Soft smile, and so forth, all her queenly boast?
Undaunted the exordium, 'I, the man
O' the people, with the people mate myself;
So stand, so fall. Kings, keep your crowns and brides!
Our progeny (if Providence agree)
Shall live to tread the bawbles underfoot,
And bid the scarecrows consort with their kin.
For son, as for his sire, be the free wife
In the free state!'"

That is, Sagacity
Would prop up one more lie, the most of all
Pernicious fancy, that the son and heir
Receives the genius from the sire, himself
Transmits as surely, — ask Experience else!
Which answers, "Never was so plain a truth
As that God drops his seed of heavenly flame
Just where he wills on earth, — sometimes where man
Seems to tempt — such the accumulated store
Of faculties — one spark to fire the heap;

Sometimes where, fire-ball-like, it falls upon
The naked unpreparedness of rock,
Burns, beaconing the nations through their night.
Faculties, fuel for the flame? All helps
Come, ought to come, or come not, crossed by chance,
From culture and transmission. What's your want
I' the son and heir? Sympathy, aptitude,
Teachableness, the fuel for the flame?
You'll have them for your pains; but the flame's self,
The novel thought of God, shall light the world?
No, poet, though your offspring rhyme and chime
I' the cradle; painter, no, for all your pet
Draws his first eye, beats Salvatore's boy;
And thrice no, statesman, should your progeny
Tie bib and tucker with no tape but red,
And make a foolscap-kite of protocols!
Critic and copyist and bureaucrat
To heart's content! The seed o' the apple-tree
Brings forth another tree which bears a crab:
'Tis the great gardener grafts the excellence
On wildings where he will."

"How plain I view,
Across those misty years 'twixt me and Rome,"
(Such the man's answer to Sagacity,)
"The little wayside temple, half way down
To a mild river that makes oxen white
Miraculously, un-mouse-colors hide,
Or so the Roman country people dream!
I view that sweet small shrub-embedded shrine
On the declivity was sacred once
To a transmuting Genius of the land
Could touch and turn its dunnest natures bright;
Since Italy means the Land of the Ox, we know.
Well, how was it the due succession fell
From priest to priest who ministered i' the cool
Calm fane o' the Clitumnian god? The sire
Brought forth a son and sacerdotal sprout,
Endowed instinctively with good and grace
To suit the gliding gentleness below,
Did he? Tradition tells another tale.
Each priest obtained his predecessor's staff,
Robe, fillet, and insignia, blamelessly,

By springing out of ambush, soon or late,
And slaying him : the initiative rite
Simply was murder, save that murder took,
I' the case, another and religious name.
So it was once, is now, shall ever be,
With genius and its priesthood in this world :
The new power slays the old, but handsomely.
There he lies, not diminished by an inch
Of stature that he graced the altar with ;
Though somebody of other bulk and build
Cries, 'What a goodly personage lies here
Reddening the water where the bulrush roots !
May I conduct the service in his place,
Decently and in order, as did he,
And, as he did not, keep a wary watch
When meditating 'neath a willow shade !'
Find out your best man ; sure the son of him
Will prove best man again, and, better still
Somehow than best, the grandson-prodigy !
You think the world would last another day,
Did we so make us masters of the trick

Whereby the works go, we could pre-arrange
Their play, and reach perfection when we please?
Depend on it, the change and the surprise
Are part o' the plan: 'tis we wish steadiness:
Nature prefers a motion by unrest,
Advancement through this force that jostles that.
And so, since much remains i' the world to see,
Here is it still, affording God the sight."
Thus did the man refute Sagacity
Ever at this one whisper in his ear:—
"Here are you picked out by a miracle,
And placed conspicuously enough, folks say,
And you believe, by Providence outright
Taking a new way—nor without success—
To put the world upon its mettle: good!
But Fortune alternates with Providence:
Resource is soon exhausted. Never count
On such a happy hit occurring twice!
Try the old method next time!"

"Old enough,"

(To whisper in his ear, the laugh outbroke,)
"And most discredited of all the modes
By just the men and women who make boast
They are kings and queens thereby! Mere self-defence
Should teach them, on one chapter of the law
Must be no sort of trifling, — chastity:
They stand or fall as their progenitors
Were chaste or unchaste. Now, run eye around
My crowned acquaintance; give each life its look,
And no more: why, you'd think each life was led
Purposely for example of what pains
Who leads it took to cure the prejudice,
And prove there's nothing so unprovable
As who is who, what son of what a sire,
And, inferentially, how faint the chance
That the next generation needs to fear
Another fool o' the selfsame type as he
Happily regnant now by right divine
And luck o' the pillow! No: select your lord
By the direct employment of your brains
As best you may: bad as the blunder prove,

A far worse evil stank beneath the sun
When some legitimate blockhead managed so
Matters, that high time was to interfere,
Though interference came from hell itself,
And not the blind mad miserable mob
Happily ruled so long by pillow-luck
And divine right; by lies, in short, not truth.
And meanwhile use the allotted minute —

One,
Two, three, four, five, — yes, five the pendule warns!
Eh? Why, this wild work wanders past all bound
And bearing! Exile, Leicester Square, the life
I' the old gay miserable time, rehearsed,
Tried on again like cast clothes, still to serve
At a pinch, perhaps? "Who's who?" was aptly asked,
Since certainly I am not I! since when?
Where is the bud-mouthed arbitress? A nod
Out-Homering Homer! Stay! — there flits the clew

I fain would find the end of! Yes: "Meanwhile,
Use the allotted minute!" Well, you see,
(Veracious and imaginary Thiers,
Who map out thus the life I might have led,
But did not, — all the worse for earth and me, —
Doff spectacles, wipe pen, shut book, decamp!)
You see 'tis easy in heroics! Plain
Pedestrian speech shall help me perorate.
Ah, if one had no need to use the tongue!
How obvious and how easy 'tis to talk
Inside the soul, a ghostly dialogue, —
Instincts with guesses, — instinct, guess, again
With dubious knowledge, half-experience; each
And all the interlocutors alike
Subordinating, — as decorum bids,
Oh, never fear! but still decisively, —
Claims from without that take too high a tone, —
("God wills this, man wants that, the dignity
Prescribed a prince would wish the other thing,") —
Putting them back to insignificance
Beside one intimatest fact, — myself

Am first to be considered, since I live
Twenty years longer, and then end, perhaps!
But, where one ceases to soliloquize,
Somehow the motives, that did well enough
I' the darkness, when you bring them into light
Are found, like those famed cave-fish, to lack eye
And organ for the upper magnitudes.
The other common creatures, of less fine
Existence, that acknowledge earth and heaven,
Have it their own way in the argument.
Yes, forced to speak, one stoops to say — one's aim
Was — what it peradventure should have been, —
To renovate a people; mend or end
That bane come of a blessing meant the world;
Inordinate culture of the sense made quick
By soul; the lust o' the flesh, lust of the eye,
And pride of life; and, consequent on these,
The worship of that prince o' the power o' the air
Who paints the cloud and fills the emptiness,
And bids his votaries, famishing for truth,
Feed on a lie.

Alack, one lies one's self
Even in the stating that one's end was truth,
Truth only, if one states as much in words!
Give me the inner chamber of the soul
For obvious easy argument! 'tis there
One pits the silent truth against a lie, —
Truth which breaks shell a careless, simple bird,
Nor wants a gorget nor a beak filed fine,
Steel spurs, and the whole armory o' the tongue,
To equalize the odds. But, do your best,
Words have to come; and, somehow, words deflect
As the best cannon ever rifled will.

So, i' the Residenz yet, not Leicester Square,
Alone, — no such congenial intercourse! —
My revery concludes, as dreaming should,
With daybreak: nothing done and over yet,
Except cigars! The adventure thus may be,
Or never needs to be at all: who knows?
My Cousin-Duke, perhaps, at whose hard head —
Is it, now — is this letter to be launched,

The sight of whose gray oblong, and whose seal,
Set all these fancies floating for an hour?

Twenty years are good gain, come what come will!
Double or quits! The letter goes! Or stays?

HERVÉ RIEL.

HERVÉ RIEL.

On the sea and at the Hogue, sixteen hundred ninety-two,
Did the English fight the French, — woe to France!
And the thirty-first of May, helter-skelter through the blue,
Like a crowd of frightened porpoises a shoal of sharks pursue,
Came crowding ship on ship to St. Malo on the Rance,
With the English fleet in view.

'Twas the squadron that escaped, with the victor in full chase:
First and foremost of the drove, in his great ship, Damfreville;
Close on him fled, great and small,
Twenty-two good ships in all;
And they signalled to the place,
"Help the winners of a race!
Get us guidance, give us harbor, take us quick; or, quicker still,
Here's the English can and will!"

Then the pilots of the place put out brisk, and leaped on board:
"Why, what hope or chance have ships like these to pass?" laughed they:
"Rocks to starboard, rocks to port, all the passage scarred and scored,
Shall the 'Formidable' here with her twelve and eighty guns
Think to make the river-mouth by the single narrow way,

Trust to enter where 'tis ticklish for a craft of twenty tons,
    And with flow at full beside?
    Now 'tis slackest ebb of tide.
  Reach the mooring? Rather say,
While rock stands, or water runs,
  Not a ship will leave the bay!"

Then was called a council straight:
Brief and bitter the debate.
"Here's the English at our heels: would you have them
      take in tow
All that's left us of the fleet, linked together stern and
      bow,
For a prize to Plymouth Sound?
Better run the ships aground!"
  (Ended Damfreville his speech.)
"Not a minute more to wait!
  Let the captains all and each
  Shove ashore, then blow up, burn the vessels on the
      beach!
France must undergo her fate."

"Give the word!" But no such word
Was ever spoke or heard:
For up stood, for out stepped, for in struck, amid all these, —
A captain? a lieutenant? a mate, — first, second, third?
No such man of mark, and meet
With his betters to compete!
But a simple Breton sailor pressed by Tourville for the fleet,
A poor coasting-pilot he, — Hervé Riel the Croisickese.

And "What mockery or malice have we here?" cries Hervé Riel.
"Are you mad, you Malouins? Are you cowards, fools, or rogues?
Talk to me of rocks and shoals? — me, who took the soundings, tell
On my fingers every bank, every shallow, every swell,
'Twixt the offing here and Grève, where the river disembogues?

Are you bought by English gold? Is it love the lying's
for?
Morn and eve, night and day,
Have I piloted your bay,
Entered free and anchored fast at the foot of Solidor.
Burn the fleet, and ruin France? That were worse
than fifty Hogues!
Sirs, they know I speak the truth! Sirs, believe
me, there's a way!
Only let me lead the line,
Have the biggest ship to steer,
Get this 'Formidable' clear,
Make the others follow mine,
And I lead them, most and least, by a passage I know
well,
Right to Solidor, past Grève,
And there lay them safe and sound;
And, if one ship misbehave, —
Keel so much as grate the ground, —
Why, I've nothing but my life: here's my head!" cries
Hervé Riel.

Not a minute more to wait.
"Steer us in, then, small and great!
  Take the helm, lead the line, save the squadron!" cried its chief.
Captains, give the sailor place!
  He is admiral, in brief.
Still the north wind, by God's grace.
See the noble fellow's face,
As the big ship, with a bound,
Clears the entry like a hound,
Keeps the passage as its inch of way were the wide sea's profound!
  See, safe through shoal and rock,
  How they follow in a flock!
Not a ship that misbehaves, not a keel that grates the ground,
  Not a spar that comes to grief!
The peril, see, is past!
All are harbored to the last!
And, just as Hervé Riel hollas "Anchor!" sure as fate,
Up the English come, — too late!

So the storm subsides to calm :
  They see the green trees wave
  On the heights o'erlooking Grève ;
Hearts that bled are stanched with balm.
"Just our rapture to enhance,
  Let the English rake the bay,
Gnash their teeth, and glare askance
  As they cannonade away!
'Neath rampired Solidor pleasant riding on the Rance!"
How hope succeeds despair on each captain's countenance!
Outburst all with one accord,
  "This is paradise for hell!
    Let France, let France's king,
    Thank the man that did the thing!"
What a shout, and all one word,
  "Hervé Riel!"
As he stepped in front once more;
  Not a symptom of surprise
  In the frank blue Breton eyes, —
Just the same man as before.

Then said Damfreville, "My friend,
I must speak out at the end,
  Though I find the speaking hard:
Praise is deeper than the lips:
You have saved the king his ships;
  You must name your own reward.
'Faith, our sun was near eclipse!
Demand whate'er you will,
France remains your debtor still.
Ask to heart's content, and have! or my name's not
    Damfreville."

Then a beam of fun outbroke
On the bearded mouth that spoke,
As the honest heart laughed through
Those frank eyes of Breton blue:—
"Since I needs must say my say;
  Since on board the duty's done,
  And from Malo Roads to Croisic Point what is it but
    a run?—

Since 'tis ask and have, I may;
  Since the others go ashore, —
Come! A good whole holiday!
  Leave to go and see my wife, whom I call the Belle Aurore!"
  That he asked, and that he got, — nothing more.

Name and deed alike are lost:
Not a pillar nor a post
  In his Croisic keeps alive the feat as it befell;
Not a head in white and black
On a single fishing-smack
In memory of the man but for whom had gone to wrack
  All that France saved from the fight whence England bore the bell.
Go to Paris; rank on rank
  Search the heroes flung pell-mell
On the Louvre, face and flank:
  You shall look long enough ere you come to Hervé Riel.

So, for better and for worse,
Hervé Riel, accept my verse!
In my verse, Hervé Riel, do thou once more
Save the squadron, honor France, love thy wife the Belle
Aurore!

www.ingramcontent.com/pod-product-compliance
Lightning Source LLC
LaVergne TN
LVHW010219110826
845151LV00004B/1136

* 9 7 8 1 4 2 5 5 2 6 8 7 0 *